Valé 12/23

START!

TO FOLLOW

How to Be a Successful
Follower of Jesus Christ

D0980710

GREG LAURIE

KERYGMA™
PUBLISHING

International Standard Book Number: 978-1-61291-296-7

Published by Kerygma Publishing

Cover design by Ross Geerdes, Creative Director, RG.Design

Coordination: FM Management, Ltd.

Contact: mark@fmmgt.net

Printed in the United States of America

1 2 3 4 5 6 7 8 / 17 16 15 14 13 12

To Jonathan Allen Laurie,
a growing disciple of Jesus Christ
of whom I am very proud.

CONTENTS

INTRODUCTION

When you hear the word *disciple*, what comes to mind? Maybe you think of the twelve disciples who tramped along behind Jesus through the Judean wilderness and the dusty streets of Jerusalem. Maybe you visualize their faces in a stained glass church window or in some old painting with little halos over their heads.

But here's the question: When you hear the word *disciple*, do you think of yourself? Do you consider yourself a disciple of Jesus Christ? Do you know what it means to be one?

True discipleship is getting back to the Christian life as it was meant to be lived. In one sense, we might call it radical Christian living. In our age of personal rights and independent thinking, discipleship might really seem like a radical concept. And when we compare it to the anemic substitute offered up by so many today as "the Christian life," it might seem really radical.

As far as the Bible is concerned, however, radical Christian living is really *normal* Christian living. The first-century believers who followed Jesus wholeheartedly were men and women who turned their world upside down. They lived the

7

Christian life as Jesus had presented it to them personally.

Here's the good news: All of this doesn't have to be ancient history. We, too, right here in the twenty-first century, can participate in this lifestyle. And that's the purpose of this little book—to call us back to *real* New Testament Christian living.

It's my conviction that every disciple is a believer, *but not every believer is necessarily a disciple.* Anything short of discipleship, however, is settling for less than what God really desires for us. When we fail to respond to His call, we fall short of His perfect will and miss out on living the Christian life as it truly was meant to be lived.

Is your life challenging? Exciting? Does it have purpose and direction? Or do you find yourself depressed, aimless, or even afraid? If your Christian experience is dull, unfulfilling, or boring, then it's time to seriously examine the statements of Jesus concerning discipleship.

What the world needs more of today is Christians who are full of joy and completely fearless.

That's a snapshot of a real disciple.

And it can be our snapshot too.

Let's find out how.

ARE YOU
HIS DISCIPLE?

The Christian life is the greatest life there is. Having lived on both sides of the fence, I can say without a doubt that it's the *better* way to live — by a million miles.

Really, there's no comparison.

As the Bible says, following Jesus means turning "from darkness to light, and from the power of Satan to God" (Acts 26:18). I wasn't brought up to pray, read the Bible, or go to church. I had pretty much experienced all the world has to offer, which sent me on a search that ultimately led me to a relationship with God through Jesus Christ.

Instead of turmoil, I found peace.

Instead of misery, I felt joy.

Instead of hate, I had love.

And most importantly, instead of a future separated from God in a place called hell, I have the strong hope and assurance of being in His presence forever in heaven.

But the Christian life is more than just praying a prayer and getting "fire insurance," so to speak. It is following Jesus

Christ not only as your Savior, but also as your Lord. It is having Him not only as your Friend, but also as your Master.

Here's the problem: There are a lot of Christians who have never grown up spiritually. They made an initial commitment to Jesus, yet they have never really understood what it means to be a committed follower of Christ. In short, they have not responded to what the Bible calls discipleship. They're still acting like spiritual toddlers in daycare.

I have two granddaughters, and so of course I think babies are cute. But I also realize that babies are a lot of work. For example, just teaching a baby how to eat is a process. When they're young, they need to be nursed or fed formula. Next, they work up to baby food and eat all that lovely strained whatever. When they get teeth, they can begin eating baby-sized bites of food that have been carefully cut up for them. Then they learn how to use a spoon and other utensils. Eventually they learn how to cut their food, eat their food, and ultimately, prepare their food.

It's called growing up.

In the same way, there are some people who have never grown up spiritually. Yet the Bible warns us, "So let us stop going over the basic teachings about Christ again and again. Let us go on instead and become mature in our understanding" (Hebrews 6:1, NLT). We need to grow up spiritually, mature as believers, and become real disciples.

REQUIREMENTS FOR A DISCIPLE

Early in His earthly ministry, Jesus called out to a tax collector named Levi (Matthew), "Follow Me" (Mark 2:14). Understanding just what Jesus meant by these words will help us get a better picture of what a disciple is. From the original Greek, "follow Me" may be better translated "follow *with* Me."

That might seem like a small distinction . . . but it is not. In fact, it's a gigantic truth, and we need to wrap our arms around it.

By saying "follow with Me," Jesus is effectively promising to be our Companion and Friend as we consistently walk the same road with Him. He's not just saying, "Okay, get in line and follow along behind Me. See you at the finish line." No, He is promising to walk with us through life—all of life, the good and the bad, the joyful and the sorrowful.

So how do we get there? What are the conditions we have to meet to be known as His disciples?

Jesus laid out the requirements in Luke 14, telling us what we need to do to really be His disciples. He addressed these words to a massive group of people who were just beginning to follow Him. But to fully understand why Jesus made the statements He did, we need to set the scene a little.

Jesus was at the peak of His popularity at this point in His ministry. Immense crowds thronged Him wherever He went. If you wanted to get near Jesus, you needed as much determination as blind Bartimaeus, who literally screamed out His name in the crowd—much to the dismay of the disciples. Or you needed the faith and persistence of the sick woman who reasoned that if she could just touch the Lord in some way, she would be healed. Or you would need the boldness of the four friends who tore a hole in the roof of the house where Jesus was speaking, lowering their sick friend right in front of His feet.

Clearly, Jesus was greatly admired for His dramatic miracles and insightful teaching. He had become enormously popular among the common people of that time, elevating the outcasts of society and assuring them of God's love while repeatedly blasting the religious hypocrites of His day.

The crowds loved it. He was the most interesting, compelling public figure to come along in years. But even though the people admired Him, that didn't necessarily mean they *followed* Him. And as He looked out on the huge multitude of observers, He could clearly see that these people really didn't know what they were doing. They really didn't have a clue as to what it meant to be His true disciples.

And that's why He challenged them . . . and us:

> "If anyone comes to Me and does not hate his father and mother, wife and children, brothers and sisters, yes, and his own life also, he cannot be My disciple. And whoever does not bear his cross and come after Me cannot be My disciple. For which of you, intending to build a tower, does not sit down first and count the cost, whether he has enough to finish it? . . . So likewise, whoever of you does not forsake all that he has cannot be My disciple." (Luke 14:26–28, 33)

Strong words, aren't they?

Jesus wasn't calling people to some lame, half-hearted belief in Him; He was looking for complete and total commitment. He was looking for people whom He could call "disciples."

And guess what? He still is.

Jesus is still asking us to step out from the multitude, from the fair-weather followers, from the fickle people to be real disciples.

He saw a problem developing that we still have with us: people who respond only to certain aspects of His message. They were picking and choosing what appealed to them and pretty much ignoring the rest, not unlike what people do today. So He determined that it was time to clearly lay out the requirements of following Him, the true cost of discipleship. Three times in this short passage, He points out that if you don't do these things, you "cannot be My disciple."

These are absolute prerequisites.

PRIORITIES FOR A DISCIPLE

Loving God more than anyone or anything else is the very foundation of being a disciple. Jesus said, "If anyone comes to Me and does not hate his father and mother, wife and children, brothers and sisters, yes, and his own life also, he cannot be My disciple" (Luke 14:26).

When we first read that, we might be a little shocked and say, "What? Is Jesus asking us to *hate* people?"

No, He is not. As we balance this verse with other Scripture, we know clearly that Jesus is not commanding us to hate people — especially members of our own family. Why would God tell us to honor our fathers and mothers in one place, and then demand that we hate them in another?

We need to get the big picture here.

What He was saying is that we should love God more than anyone or anything else — so much so that our love for those people or things would seem like hatred in comparison.

It makes perfect sense when you think about it. If you want to live your Christian life to its fullest, then love Jesus more than anyone or anything else.

People have been kept back from following Jesus by their fear of what others might think. They know that if they give their life to Christ, they will lose a lot of so-called friends. If they give their life to Christ, it would mean the end of a relationship. If they give their life to Christ, it would cause friction in their home. That is what holds them back. But Jesus is saying, "If you really want to be My disciple, *you must love Me more than anyone or anything else.*"

Here is what it comes down to: Either you will have harmony with God and friction with people, or you will have harmony with people and friction with God.

If you are living the way that God wants you to live, then it is inevitable that some people in your life will be bothered or offended by that commitment. You need to know that right up front. Jesus said, "Woe to you when everyone speaks well of you, for that is how their ancestors treated the false prophets" (Luke 6:26, NIV).

If you are really a follower of Jesus Christ and living as you ought to, there will be certain people who don't like you for that reason alone. Don't let it throw you. Don't be hurt or offended by that. You need to understand that it's par for the course. As Jesus said, "'A servant is not greater than his master.' If they persecuted me, they will persecute you also" (John 15:20, NIV).

A disciple loves God more than anyone or anything else.

THE CROSS AND THE DISCIPLE

Jesus underscored the importance of commitment on the part of a disciple when He referred to the cross. He said, "Whoever does not bear his cross and come after Me cannot be My disciple" (Luke 14:27), and "If anyone desires to come after Me, let him deny himself, and take up his cross daily, and follow Me. For whoever desires to save his life will lose it, but whoever loses his life for My sake will save it" (Luke 9:23–24).

Today, the cross has been largely stripped of its original meaning. Shrouded in tradition, it has become a symbol of many things, from a religious icon to an ornate piece of jewelry studded in diamonds or pearls. Yet the real cross of history was a hated, despised symbol — the symbol of a cruel and barbaric death. The Romans reserved this form of torture and execution for the lowest of criminals.

Today we wouldn't expect to see many diamond-studded guillotines or sterling silver electric chairs hanging around people's necks.

"What's that around your neck?"

"Oh, it's a little gurney — like where they strap people down and give them a lethal injection."

"Oh . . . how nice."

These are symbols of death, symbols of shame. The cross was the same thing. When a man carried his cross down the streets of Jerusalem, it was well-known that he was about to die. The convicted criminal would be driven outside the city, nailed to that cross, and placed by the roadside where everyone coming in and out of the city would see him.

So when Jesus said, "If anyone desires to come after Me, let him . . . take up his cross," it was more than a little shocking to His listeners. He intentionally chose an attention-getting, even despicable, symbol of torture and rejection to illustrate what it means to follow Him. The cross symbolizes one thing: death. And in this context, it means dying to self.

Sometimes people identify whatever problem, difficult relationship, or obstacle they have as their "cross to bear." But that is not what bearing the cross means. *For disciples, it means that wherever Jesus directs, they should be willing to go.*

Obviously, this isn't an appealing message to many. Satan made an accurate statement of humanity when he said, "All that a man has he will give for his life" (Job 2:4). In other words, the enemy knows that when the chips are down, people will give up everything to stay alive, to preserve themselves.

Jesus was definitely not advocating what I call easy believism. Far too often we hear, "Just ask Jesus into your heart. He'll make you a happier person. Let God be your copilot." Some will falsely assert that you will become wealthier or healthier once you are a Christian. But that is not the Christianity of the New Testament.

God doesn't offer Himself to us as some celestial big brother or good buddy. The bottom line is that God is absolutely holy and perfect, and we have all sinned horribly against Him. But God, in His great love, bridged the tremendous gap that sin produced, and He sent His own dear Son to die on the cross for us. To receive Him into our lives, we must not only believe in Him, but we must also turn from our sins and follow Him as both our Savior and Lord.

To deny yourself, take up the cross daily, and follow Jesus Christ flies in the face of self-love, which is widely accepted today, even in the church. We hear a great deal about "self-worth," "self-image," and "self-esteem," yet this shouldn't surprise us, because the Bible warns us that narcissistic attitudes will be prevalent in the days before Christ's return:

But mark this: There will be terrible times in the last days. People will be *lovers of themselves*, lovers of money, boastful, proud, abusive, disobedient to their parents, ungrateful, unholy, without love, unforgiving, slanderous, without self-control, brutal, not lovers of the good, treacherous, rash, conceited, lovers of pleasure rather than lovers of God — having a form of godliness but denying its power. (2 Timothy 3:1–5, NIV, emphasis added)

What an accurate description of our times. As we look at our nation and see a society coming apart at the seams, we must realize that America's only hope is a nationwide revival.

God gives us His recipe for revival in 2 Chronicles 7:14: "If My people who are called by My name will humble themselves, and pray and seek My face, and turn from their wicked ways, then I will hear from heaven, and will forgive their sin and heal their land."

One of the first conditions we must meet to see our sins forgiven and our land healed is found in the beginning of this passage: "If my people . . . pray." Of the twelve Hebrew words employed to express the single verb "to pray," the one used here means "to judge self habitually" — not to love yourself or to esteem yourself but to judge yourself . . . habitually.

This is what Jesus means when He tells us to deny ourselves. Discipleship involves commitment. Although discipline isn't an appealing word or idea for many of us, it's essential to being a disciple of Jesus Christ. It requires setting aside our aims, goals, ambitions, or desires in life. It involves giving up our own will and rights.

Jesus underscored this when He said, "So likewise, whoever of you does not forsake all that he has cannot be My disciple" (Luke 14:33). This doesn't mean that to live the life of a disciple, you have to take a vow of poverty and give everything away. Jesus meant that we are to surrender our claim to our possessions. In other words, we are not to be possessed by possessions.

The only obsession a disciple should have is with Jesus Christ. *He* must be the most important pursuit in our lives. He must be more important than our career or our personal happiness. In fact, we never will find personal happiness until we are fully committed to Christ. Personal happiness is a by-product of knowing Him: "Happy are the people whose God is the LORD!" (Psalm 144:15).

The truth is that when you die to yourself, you find yourself. When you lay aside personal goals, desires, and ambitions, that is when God will reveal the desires, ambitions, and goals that He has for you. And they're better ones than you could ever come up with on your own. This is what the apostle Paul meant when he said, "I have been crucified with Christ; it is no longer I who live, but Christ lives in me" (Galatians 2:20).

Are you bearing the cross right now and following Jesus? For some people, it may mean the suffering of persecution. It may mean a major change in lifestyle. It may cost them friends. To others it could even mean dying for the faith. Whatever the case, bearing the cross will affect and influence every aspect of a person's life.

Until we recognize that everything we have belongs to Jesus, we are not His disciples. If we are aware of God's will for our lives but unwilling to go in the direction God wants us to go, then we are not His disciples.

FROM CURIOUS TO COMMITTED

In his insightful book on discipleship, J. Dwight Pentecost writes about the idea of radical Christian living, or true discipleship. He sums it up in three simple words: *curious*, *convinced*, and *committed.*

When Jesus performed His first miracle, or sign, of turning water into wine, the disciples had gone from curious to convinced—convinced that He was an extraordinary person, perhaps even the Messiah: "This beginning of signs Jesus did in Cana of Galilee, and manifested His glory; and His disciples believed in Him" (John 2:11).

When we first see or hear of Jesus Christ, we're curious. Listening to what He said, learning of His life and the miracles attributed to Him, and hearing what others say about Him are obvious attractions—just as they were for the multitudes that surrounded Him when He walked this earth. But there comes a time when we must step over the line of being curious to becoming convinced. And I would venture to say that many who attend church today have never really crossed that line. They are curious, but nothing more. They are attracted to the message, and maybe even to the Christian life, but they aren't fully convinced it's true.

These people are like the multitudes after Jesus fed the five thousand with only five loaves of bread and two fish. After He performed this miracle, His popularity soared. Word on the street probably was that if you wanted a free meal, then follow Jesus of Nazareth. There's no doubt that thousands came to hear Him speak, but many were most likely there because of their empty stomachs—not their empty hearts. They were interested in Jesus' message as long as it took care of their temporary needs and as long as it was convenient, which became clear in their response to His message.

After Jesus gave a very difficult series of teachings on commitment and sacrifice, these so-called followers were repulsed by it and turned away. Then Jesus turned to His disciples and asked if they wanted to leave also.

Peter responded, "Lord, to whom shall we go? You have the words of eternal life. Also we have come to believe and know that You are the Christ, the Son of the living God" (John 6:68–69). The curious went home, but the convinced stuck with Him.

But something more needed to be developed in their belief. They needed to go from being convinced to being committed.

At Caesarea Philippi, Jesus asked the disciples, "Who do men say that I, the Son of Man, am?" (Matthew 16:13). They replied that many thought Jesus to be John the Baptist, while others thought He might be Elijah or even Jeremiah.

Then Jesus asked, "But who do you say that I am?" (verse 15).

Up to this point, the answers He'd heard were those of the curious. Then a convinced disciple named Simon Peter stood up and made a step toward being committed. He replied, "You are the Christ, the Son of the living God" (verse 16). Peter had passed from being curious and convinced to being totally and completely committed.

Where do you stand? Are you merely curious? Or perhaps even convinced? Have you made that step of faith to become committed? You become a disciple in the biblical sense only when you are totally and completely committed to Jesus Christ and His Word.

THE RESULTS OF DISCIPLESHIP

John's Gospel contains three important verses that will help us understand what it means to be a disciple. They provide us with three evidences, or results, of discipleship.

Result 1: You will bear fruit. *"By this My Father is glorified, that you bear much fruit; so you will be My disciples"* (John 15:8).

This is what you might call a cornerstone verse in the New Testament. Jesus is saying here that if you are true disciple, you *will* bear fruit. This means your life will display practical results as you follow Jesus.

Result 2: You will study and obey God's Word. *"If you abide in My word, you are My disciples indeed"* (John 8:31).

If you are a true disciple, then you will study and obey God's Word. Disciples of Jesus will be students of Scripture and will walk according to its teaching.

Result 3: You will love one another. *"By this all will know that you are My disciples, if you have love for one another"* (John 13:35).

As a true disciple, your life won't only be characterized by practical results and a hunger for Scripture, but you also will have love for others—especially fellow believers. Without all of these characteristics, you can't really claim to be His disciple.

COMMITMENT IS KEY

Are you His disciple today? Perhaps you're still just curious, or only slightly convinced. Maybe you are convinced but haven't overcome that final hurdle of commitment. Until you reach that point, you can't truly be called His disciple.

A true disciple who desires to live a radical Christian life must anchor himself in Romans 12:1: "I beseech you therefore, brethren, by the mercies of God, that you present your bodies a living sacrifice, holy, acceptable to God, which is your reasonable service."

In the Jewish wedding ceremony, the moment at which the father of the bride gave his daughter's hand to the bridegroom was called the presentation. In the same way, God wants us to present ourselves to Him.

Paul, in the chapters leading up to Romans 12, outlines all that God had done for us. Now he is saying, "In light of all this, I urge you, by the mercies of God, because of what He has done for you, to present yourself to Him as a living sacrifice." Paul's idea of discipleship isn't just giving mental acknowledgment to Jesus as God — head knowledge. No, he is saying that this includes obedience and sacrifice.

The requirements of discipleship are different from the requirements of salvation. To be a Christian, you need to believe in Jesus Christ, whom God sent, and then you will receive eternal life through Him. It's a *gift*. To be a disciple is to take up the cross daily and follow Him, making His will your will. It's a *commitment.*

Jesus is looking for disciples, not just people who are Christians in name only. Jesus has plenty of fair-weather followers today, people who follow Him when it's convenient, when it's socially or economically advantageous, or when they're in the mood. But when a crisis, persecution, or difficulty comes, they throw in the towel and turn away.

Every disciple is a Christian, but not every Christian is necessarily a disciple. Do you want to be more than curious about Jesus — and more than convinced? Then commit your life to Him as a disciple and discover what radical Christian living is all about!

Perhaps a commitment like this seems too difficult right now. But remember this: If God asks you to do something, He will give you the strength to do it. God's calling is God's enabling. As Philippians 2:13 tells us, "For it is God who works in you both to will and to do for His good pleasure."

That is our guarantee. God will be our enabler. It doesn't take great knowledge. It doesn't take great ability. It doesn't take great willpower. It only takes our availability.

TRAITS OF
A DISCIPLE

We need people today who walk and talk with Jesus Christ, people who, before they even speak a single word, give evidence that there is something different about their lives. We need people who, through their godly lifestyles, have earned the right to be heard.

Another way to say it? What we need today are people who have been with Jesus.

Let's say that you saw a man whose face was bright red. You might ask him, "Were you in the sun recently?" Why would you ask that? Because you see the *evidence* on his face. In the same way, people need to see the evidence of Christ in our lives. They should be able to tell that we have been with Him.

Could that be said of you? Could someone look at you and your lifestyle—your attitude, your words, and your facial expressions—and say, "He's been with Jesus" or "She's been with Jesus"? Could people tell that you're a follower of Jesus Christ by the way you treat others? By the way you act around your family? By your outlook on life?

ABIDING

As we noted in the last chapter, the first result of discipleship is that you will bear fruit.

But how? How does that happen?

We find the answer in John 15:4, where Jesus says plainly that for this to take place, we must abide in Him: "Abide in Me, and I in you. As the branch cannot bear fruit of itself, unless it abides in the vine, neither can you, unless you abide in Me."

So what does it mean to abide? It's much the same as following Christ: walking with Him consistently as our Lord and our friend. But it takes the idea even further. To abide means that we're sinking our roots deep into a love relationship with Jesus. It's not simply walking with and serving Him when it's easy, convenient, or popular. *When we abide in Christ, we remain in fellowship with Him daily, regardless of outward circumstances or inner emotions.*

In this verse, Jesus used the analogy of a vine to describe the importance of abiding. It causes us to think of vegetation that draws its strength from the soil. If we were to uproot a tree and move it to another area, then after a while uproot it again and move it to yet a different place, it's quite possible we would damage that tree. And if we repeated the process several more times, the tree would almost certainly die.

Yet that is exactly how many men and women try to live their Christian lives: rooting and uprooting . . . rooting and uprooting. Some believers have never found a place of *consistency* in their walk with God. Often they are the ones who respond again and again to invitations to receive Christ. They find themselves in a continual cycle of making "commitments" to Christ, but quickly falling away when they face the pressures and temptations of the real world.

King David once wrote, "Create in me a clean heart, O God, and renew a steadfast spirit within me" (Psalm 51:10). A steadfast spirit also could be translated a *consistent* spirit. So to bear fruit, we must consistently sink our roots deeply into a relationship with Jesus Christ and walk with Him.

Real spiritual growth comes only through discipline and perseverance. In other words, it comes through sticking with it. One of the traps for all of us, however, is substituting activity for genuine fellowship with God.

I'm reminded of the story of Mary and Martha in Luke 10. These two sisters had invited Jesus and His disciples into their home for a meal. Martha wanted to whip up a feast for a king (literally) and worked herself into a frenzy to pull off a five-star banquet. Her sister Mary, however, got so caught up in what Jesus was saying that she forgot all about the meal and helping her sister. She sat down at Jesus' feet, hanging on every word He said.

The meal, of course, was important—a love gift from Martha's heart. But it wasn't nearly as important as cashing in on the opportunity to be close to Jesus.

Mary is the picture of a disciple who has learned the importance of listening, while Martha is the picture of many Christians today. In our chaotic world, we can easily identify with Martha as we often must choose between a certain activity and setting aside time to spend with God. And like Martha, when we fail to sit at the feet of Jesus, we usually end up frustrated.

There's no doubt that Martha had the best of intentions. She wanted to please the Lord by what she did and how she performed. But Mary wanted to be as close to Him as she could get and not miss a word. Yes, there is a time to be active in serving God, but before we can effectively work *for* Him, we need to first learn to wait *on* Him. Before we can *give out* to others, we must *take in* for ourselves. Before we can disciple others, we must learn for ourselves what it means to be a disciple. A disciple always takes time to sit at the feet of Jesus.

The attitude of a real disciple would be similar to that of a passenger on a plane that is about to attempt an emergency landing on a freeway or a river. Would you pay close attention to the captain's voice on the intercom at a time like that? Would you listen carefully to the flight attendant's instructions about how to use your seat as a flotation device?

Oh yes, you would!

In fact, you would hang on every word.

You would forget all about the in-flight movie, that game of solitaire you had been playing on your computer, or that crossword puzzle in the airline magazine. In that situation, listening could mean life or death.

That is how Mary listened to Jesus, and that is how we should listen as well. She learned the secret of abiding, and we need to learn it as well—if we truly want to be His disciples.

"THEY HAD BEEN WITH JESUS"

In the book of Acts, we find another story of two disciples, Peter and John, who had spent time with Jesus and had been radically impacted by their relationship with Him. As a result, they wanted to tell as many people as possible about it, which led to their being arrested and brought before the Sanhedrin, the Jewish leadership council in Jerusalem.

It was a source of amazement to these religious leaders

that ordinary fishermen — regular guys off the street, so to speak — were so well-versed in the Scriptures and, more importantly, in the understanding of them. They appeared to have more understanding of the Word of God than even the rabbis, the trained professionals. How could this be? Acts 4:13 provides the answer: "They [the religious leaders] realized that they had been with Jesus."

These two men were present on the Day of Pentecost, when the power of God had dramatically fallen. A sound like a mighty rushing wind had filled the room, and divided flames of fire rested upon each disciple as they had been waiting for this "power from on high" (Luke 24:49).

Pentecost was now over, and those little flames were no longer visible over the heads of the disciples — but they were replaced by burning hearts. So Peter and John, with hearts aflame, were headed over to the temple to pray one day. It was 3:00 p.m. on an ordinary day. We don't read of an angel instructing them to go to the temple because a miracle would be performed, nor do we read of a pillar of fire going before them and leading them to their destination. In fact, it was a day like any other day. They didn't know what God was about to do.

As Peter and John made their way to the temple, they passed by the Beautiful Gate where a lame man was sitting and begging, probably a fixture outside the temple. He may have had his friends carry him there and strategically position him to be seen by people coming from a prayer service, no doubt hoping that God had softened their hearts toward a man in need. I wonder if people had stopped noticing him after a while. Maybe they even stepped over him as they went on their way.

On this day in Jerusalem, however, the supernatural invaded the natural. God decided to shake things up a little. Simon Peter did not, in and of himself, have the faith to do what he was about to do. God gave Peter a special measure of faith, enabling him to say to the man, "Silver and gold I do not have, but what I do have I give you: In the name of Jesus Christ of Nazareth, rise up and walk" (Acts 3:6).

But Peter didn't stop there. He took the man by his hand and helped him stand to his feet. This was another sink-or-swim moment for Peter—just like when he stepped out of the boat on that stormy night and went walking on the water toward Jesus. This would be either a great victory or a horrible disaster. Peter was going for broke, as he often did.

As he pulled the lame man to his feet, "instantly the man's feet and ankles became strong. He jumped to his feet and began to walk. Then he went with them into the temple courts, walking and jumping, and praising God" (Acts 3:7–8, NIV).

As people began to realize what had happened, that this was the same man who had sat begging by the Beautiful Gate, they began to gather around the three men. It was a ready-made congregation, and Peter took the opportunity to boldly declare the name of His Lord.

This, however, didn't play well with everyone in the temple. Some of the Jewish leaders had the temple police apprehend Peter and John and throw them in jail. The next day, the two were brought before the Sanhedrin, which included Annas and Caiaphas, both with responsibility for the crucifixion of Jesus.

These guys probably had concluded that once Jesus was dead, their problem was over. But then . . . along came Peter and John, doing mighty miracles in His name. They thought they had destroyed the Christian faith by killing Christ, yet what they didn't understand was they had played right into the plan and purpose of God. Jesus was living in each of His followers.

This story, among other things, shows us how God can use ordinary people in extraordinary ways.

FOUR MARKS OF AN EFFECTIVE DISCIPLE

Have you been with Jesus? These four elements working in the lives of the disciples caused them to turn their world upside down.

1. A person who has been with Jesus will boldly share his or her faith. Just months earlier, this same Peter had denied Jesus and was ashamed of Him. Now Peter was seemingly fearless, speaking with the same boldness that Jesus Himself spoke with. That is the way it works. When you spend time with Jesus, you become more like Him.

Sometimes when couples have been married for a long time, they begin to take on one another's traits. They can finish each other's sentences. They know how their spouse will react to this or to that. My wife and I have often joked that between the two of us, we have one complete brain. When you are around someone a lot, you become more and more like them.

God's objective in the life of the believer is to make you into the image of Jesus Christ. He wants you to become more and more like Him each and every day. Romans 8:29 says, "God knew his people in advance, and he chose them to become like his Son, so that his Son would be the firstborn among many brothers and sisters" (NLT).

The name *Christian* isn't one that followers of Jesus came up with. It was a description given to them by their critics, because it meant they were like Jesus. A literal translation would be, "They were of the party of Christ." Are you in the party of Christ? Or are you ashamed to be identified with Jesus? The religious leaders of the first century realized there was no stopping the Christians because they had been with Jesus. Can people recognize that about you?

2. A person who has been with Jesus will know Scripture. One thing that so amazed the Jewish leadership was Peter's grasp and knowledge of Scripture. As you read through his sermon (see Acts 3:12–26), note the number of times he quotes from various Old Testament passages. It shows us that when you have been with Jesus, you will spend time in His Word.

The Bible is the autobiography of God. It tells you everything you need to know about God, about life, and about yourself. It tells you how to live, what to do, and what not to do. It tells you how to think, how to act, and how to react. If you want to get closer to God, then you have to study the Bible.

3. A person who has been with Jesus will be a person of prayer. After being released and told to no longer preach their message, Peter and John joined the other disciples. And what did they do? They held a prayer meeting (see Acts 4:23–31), which gave them even more boldness.

4. A person who has been with Jesus will be persecuted. Peter and John were arrested, just as Jesus had been arrested before them. It's the same with us. If we allow Jesus to live His life and speak His words through us, we can expect to be treated like Jesus by our culture—which probably means we won't win many popularity contests. If everyone likes you, if everyone thinks you're wonderful, if you don't have an enemy anywhere, then something is wrong with you.

One popular Bible paraphrase puts it like this:

> There's trouble ahead when you live only for the approval of others, saying what flatters them, doing what indulges them. Popularity contests are not truth contests—look how many scoundrel preachers were approved by your ancestors! Your task is to be true, not popular. (Luke 6:26, MSG)

Does that surprise you? Maybe you have thought the opposite, that if you are a Christian, then everything should be sweetness and light and everyone will love you. There is some truth to that. You should be a loving, sweet, and kind person. But you also have to be a godly, truthful, and righteous person, and that definitely will bother certain people. People who don't believe in absolute truth can work themselves into a rage over people who *do* believe in absolute truth.

The fact is, you can tell a lot about a person by their enemies and friends. If you are really walking with Jesus, then you will face persecution. And if you are a true believer, then persecution won't weaken you, but only strengthen you. If you are not a true believer, then you will abandon what little faith you have.

Then again, sometimes we may find ourselves being persecuted simply because we act like jerks. We're obnoxious, unnecessarily offensive, or behave like self-righteous, insensitive fools. When people naturally turn away from us, we console ourselves with the thought that we are being "persecuted for Jesus' sake."

Maybe so, maybe not. Just maybe we are being rejected simply because we are behaving like idiots and don't know how to love people or be compassionate. The gospel has enough built-in offense. Let's not make it worse. Let's deliver it with compassion.

If for you, the Christian life is all about feeling good and having everything go your way, then you won't like being a disciple. Being a follower of Christ is the most joyful and exciting life there is. But it also can be the most challenging life there is. It's a life lived out under the command of someone other than yourself.

Just as soldiers receive and carry out orders from their commanding officer, we must respond to the orders of our commander-in-chief, Jesus Christ. The Bible says, "You therefore must endure hardship as a good soldier of Jesus Christ" (2 Timothy 2:3). Soldiers have made a commitment to serve and protect their country, so they respond to the orders they are given. They don't argue with their commanding officer. (They'd better not!)

In the same way, disciples have made a commitment to serve Jesus Christ and need to be willing to respond to Him when He leads them. They do what He tells them to do, go where He tells them to go, and say what He wants them to say. And more and more, they become like Him until the day they see Him face-to-face.

May God help us to be like the first-century believers and turn our world upside down in the midst of persecution, challenges, and temptation.

And may people who meet us recognize that we have been with Jesus.

THE COSTS OF DISCIPLESHIP

One of the reasons the Christians of the first century turned their world upside down in such a dramatic way was their sense of abandon. God would say to Peter, "Reach down, take that lame man's hand, and pull him to his feet," and he would do it (see Acts 3:6–7). God would tell Philip, "Go to the desert," and he would go (see Acts 8:26–27). They were willing to take risks, stepping out in obedience even when they didn't understand all the whys and wherefores.

In committing to be a disciple, one of the factors you must consider is the cost. There is a price tag associated with following Jesus.

Too often, a would-be disciple desires God's best but fails to pay the price to attain it. How can we be willing to give so little to the One who gave so much for us? He gave everything to us, and He expects nothing less in return.

Many believers are like the farmer who was known for his stinginess. When his cow gave birth to two calves, he looked at them and said, "Lord, I'm so thankful for this blessing that I'm going to give You one of my calves." He proudly told his wife of his decision, which surprised her given his normally selfish ways.

When she asked him which calf he was planning to give to the Lord, he replied, "I'm not sure yet."

Time went by, and one of the calves began to get sick. A few days later, the farmer came out of the barn, the lifeless calf draped over his arms, and sorrowfully announced, "Honey, I've got bad news. The Lord's calf just died."

In the same way, some Christians give God what they no longer want. But that is not the attitude we should have. How we miss out! How we misunderstand! God doesn't want our leftovers. He deserves the best we have. He has given so much to us that we should want to give everything we have back to Him.

"SHE DID WHAT SHE COULD"

We see this modeled by Mary—the same Mary who sat at the feet of Jesus while Martha hurried to prepare a meal for Him. Later, in another account, we find her offering Jesus the most precious thing she probably owned. In fact, she did something so outstanding, so significant, that Jesus said, "Assuredly, I say to you, wherever this gospel is preached in the whole world, what this woman has done will also be told as a memorial to her" (Mark 14:9).

By this time in the life and ministry of Jesus, He had already had a number of confrontations with the religious leaders. Bottom line, they wanted Him dead and out of the way. But how could they arrest Him or kill Him when Jerusalem was overflowing with pilgrims who had arrived for the Passover celebration? Jesus still had His admirers, and the religious leaders were afraid that if they laid hands on Him, the people might start a riot.

So while the forces of darkness were plotting, planning, and muttering behind closed doors, Jesus decided to share a meal with friends and followers at the house of Simon the leper. Presumably this was Simon the *healed* leper. Lazarus was there, who had been resurrected from the dead. His sisters Martha and Mary were present, as were the other apostles.

At some point during this visit with Jesus, Mary did something unexpected and very unusual. She took some special and costly perfume, broke open the flask, and poured it on the head of Jesus. The perfume was called spikenard, and presumably it would have been imported from India. Most likely it was a family heirloom and worth a lot of money.

It would have been one thing to sprinkle a few drops on Him, which was culturally acceptable at that time. But Mary wanted something more.

Mary wanted to do something outstanding, significant, and even extravagant to show her deep love for Jesus. So she poured *the whole bottle* on Him.

Not everyone appreciated her sacrifice. The Bible says, "Some of those present were saying indignantly to one another, 'Why this waste of perfume? It could have been sold for more than a year's wages and the money given to the poor.' And they rebuked her harshly" (Mark 14:4–5, NIV).

In other words, was such an extravagant gesture really necessary? Wasn't it just a little "over the top"? Besides, it just didn't add up to good stewardship . . . did it?

This is typical of so many people today. Like dutiful Pharisees, they will give only what is required by God. They want to get by with the bare minimum. They will ask questions like, "Can I do this or that and still be a Christian?"

In essence, they are trying to figure out the bare minimum they can give to God. Sure, they will pray briefly before a meal or before going to sleep—if they remember. They will read the Bible—if they can make time in their busy schedule. They will give something to the Lord's work—if they have a little spare change in their pocket. They will sing the worship songs in church—as long as the worship leaders don't get carried away.

So what was the inspiration behind this sense of abandon and sacrifice in Mary? It was Jesus Himself. Her idea was that nothing is too good for the Lord. And what could be wrong with that?

Jesus both defended and commended Mary for her sacrificial act:

> Why are you bothering her? She has done a beautiful thing to me. The poor you will always have with you, and you can help them any time you want. But you will not always have me. She did what she could. She poured perfume on my body beforehand to prepare for my burial. (Mark 14:6–8, NIV)

Mary "did what she could" because she understood that Jesus would do what He did. If we, like Mary, know anything of what God has done for us, then we will want to do more for Him. Nothing is ever wasted when it's done from a right motive for the glory of God.

No, you can't do everything, but you can do something.

You can't win all of the people in the world to Christ, but you can win some. *So do what you can.*

We all have something that we can do. And we must all do what we can while we can. Shouldn't we give Him the finest that we have to offer? Doesn't Jesus deserve our best?

One day your life will come to an end. And if you are conscious and aware in those final days and hours, you can be assured you never will regret having gone to church too much. You won't regret spending too much time reading and studying your Bible. You won't regret taking a few risks and sharing your faith with others. What you *will* regret is that you didn't do these things more.

SELLING OUT FOR SO LITTLE

The Bible makes it clear that we are not our own. We have been bought with a price, and therefore we are to glorify God with everything we are (see 1 Corinthians 6:19–20). As believers, we just need to let this sink in.

We don't belong to ourselves.

We don't own our own lives.

We don't own our own time.

We don't own our own money.

We don't own our own bodies.

We don't own our own possessions.

We don't own our own gifts and talents.

These things simply don't belong to us anymore, except as stewards who are expected to manage them for the Lord's use. We have to seriously consider all of this when we are committing to discipleship.

I heard about a remarkable method hunters in Africa have used to catch monkeys. They take a coconut and cut a little hole large enough for a monkey to reach into — but not large enough for it to pull its fist out. Next, they hollow out the coconut, put some warm rice inside, and place them under trees where their nets are hanging. Then the hunters wait.

When the monkeys smell the rice, they reach inside the coconuts. But the hunters have learned that the monkeys will not open their fist to let go of the rice, and therefore can't get the coconut off. When the monkeys start banging the coconuts on the ground in frustration, the hunters arrive and easily capture them. Even as the monkeys see the nets, they *still* won't let go of the coconuts, because they want the rice. As a result, they are trapped.

Many people live their whole lives for their handful of rice: a handful of possessions . . . pursuits . . . pleasures. They give up what God could do in their lives in exchange for fleeting, temporal things. Like Esau, they sell everything for a bowl of stew (see Genesis 25:29–34).

WHAT (OR WHO) IS HOLDING YOU BACK?

Discipleship not only requires *giving* our best, but it also requires *giving up* anything that would hinder us in our commitment to follow Christ. Hebrews 12:1–2 tells us,

> Therefore, since we are surrounded by such a huge crowd of witnesses to the life of faith, let us strip off every weight that slows us down, especially the sin that so easily trips us up. And let us run with endurance the race God has set before us. We do this by keeping our eyes on Jesus, the champion who initiates and perfects our faith. Because of the joy awaiting him, he endured the cross,

disregarding its shame. Now he is seated in the place of honor beside God's throne. (NLT)

As we seek to walk with Christ, we can sometimes travel with too much weight. We drag things along that shouldn't even be in our lives. It might be something we are doing that is slowing us down or it might be someone we are spending time with. But we need to get rid of excess weight.

Whenever my friend Franklin Graham visits, he wants to go for a run. He will say, "Come on, Greg. Let's go for a run in the morning!"

"Umm, okay," I say. "Looking forward to that."

Franklin is a good runner. He is disciplined. He can run consistently for a good forty-five minutes, sometimes nearly an hour. I, on the other hand, am good for about four minutes. Then I'm tired. So we will start running. As I start to slow down, Franklin will say, "Greg, come on! Greg! Greg, run!" So I will run a little bit more.

"I'm just going to walk," I will tell him after a while.

"Come on! Run!" he says.

"I *am* running," I tell him. "In my heart, I am running with you."

I think Franklin realizes that I slow him down. He is trying to run a race, and I am impeding his performance.

We have people in our lives who can have the same effect on us spiritually. When we are around them, they slow us down because they don't have the same interest in the things of God that we do.

We'll say, "Hey, let's go to church today!"

"Oh, I don't know. It's raining. It is so dangerous with the rain. Do you want to go to the mall instead?"

They drag us down, and we know it.

That is why Paul advised Timothy, "Run from anything that stimulates youthful lusts. Instead, pursue righteous living, faithfulness, love, and peace. Enjoy the companionship of those who call on the Lord with pure hearts" (2 Timothy 2:22, NLT). Spend time with people who have the same commitment to discipleship as you do — not those who will drag you down.

UNDERSTAND THE TERMS

To count the cost is to understand the terms of the commitment. How much are you willing to give?

In our pursuit to become disciples, we make decisions every day that will either encourage or discourage our spiritual growth. When we get up in the morning, it is either the news or the Bible. On the weekend, it is either sleeping in or going to church. In dealing with others, it is either harboring a grudge or choosing to forgive. When thinking about the future, it is either worrying or praying. With each choice, we will either progress or regress, advance or retreat in our quest to be His disciples.

If you look back at this point in your life and have a number of regrets, you can't change that. But you *can* change what you do today and what you will do tomorrow. You can change your course if need be.

Every hour, every minute you have given to serve Jesus, every resource you have invested, and every thought you have given over to His Word are not wasted.

They are the best possible investments.

In fact, they will last forever.

DISCIPLESHIP AND THE BIBLE

It always amazes me to see how much care and cultivation it takes to make flowers grow. My wife loves to plant flowers. She can spend hours pulling weeds, driving out snails, and working the soil.

Yet even after all that labor, how quickly and easily weeds can sprout up and take over. It seems a weed can bloom in the middle of a street or a crack in the sidewalk, and without any caretaker or special watering, it does just fine. But the delicate, vulnerable flowers require constant attention.

This is a classic illustration of the contrast between a believer's new nature and old nature. If we want to be closer to Christ and live a life pleasing to Him, we need to cultivate and nurture our new nature. The moment we stop strengthening and building up the new nature is the very moment the old one will come back to haunt us—just like a weed growing in the street.

It takes very little encouragement for our old nature to cause us trouble. All we need to do is neglect the new nature.

As the apostle Paul wrote, "I say then: Walk in the Spirit, and you shall not fulfill the lust of the flesh" (Galatians 5:16). There are disciplines every believer must maintain if he or she wants to live the Christian life as it was meant to be lived.

THE KEY TO SPIRITUAL PROGRESS

In this chapter, we will examine the first of these disciplines, found in John 8:31, where Jesus said, "If you abide in My word, you are My disciples indeed." If you and I want to truly be disciples of Jesus Christ, then we must continue to abide in — or stay attached to — the Word of God.

To a great measure, success or failure in the Christian life depends on how much of God's Word we get into our hearts and minds on a regular basis and how obedient we are to it. Everything we need to know about God is taught in the Bible. If we neglect the study of Scripture, then our spiritual life ultimately will fall into disrepair.

The Bible is the most amazing document ever given to man. Technically speaking, it is not one book but sixty-six books written over a 1,600-year period of time by everyone from kings to peasants, from philosophers to fishermen, and from poets to statesmen. Each of them was inspired by God to write down His words. They were not the authors; God was. He breathed each word.

Why is it, then, that so many believers fail to open their Bibles? Could it be that many Christians simply lack that spiritual hunger for the truth? One way for a doctor to know whether a person is healthy is to check his or her appetite. When there isn't any appetite, it usually means something is wrong. In the same way, some Christians don't have an appetite for the Word of God. Some see reading God's Word as a duty, a drudgery, an obligation. But that can change when they begin to see the real, observable differences it makes in their relationships and in their daily lives.

Hungry Christians are healthy Christians. The Bible tells us, "Like newborn babies, crave pure spiritual milk, so that by it you may grow up in your salvation, now that you have tasted that the Lord is good" (1 Peter 2:2–3, NIV). To crave the pure milk of the Word means that we intensely long for the teaching of the Bible because we want to grow. If we are not making progress spiritually, then it's very possible that we aren't yearning for the Scriptures.

The prophet Hosea's cry is still relevant: "My people are destroyed for lack of knowledge" (Hosea 4:6). Today, many believers throw in the towel, fall into sin, or are misled by false teachings because they have never developed the vital discipline of studying the Bible on a regular basis. If we are to be disciples of Jesus Christ, leading effective and successful Christian lives, then God's Word must be a priority.

Proverbs 2:1–9 provides a wonderful series of promises that will help us get the most from our study of Scripture. For every promise, there is a condition that we must fulfill. The conditions listed in the first five verses state that we must receive His words and treasure His commandments, cry out for discernment, and seek understanding as though we were mining for gold.

KNOW THE BIBLE FOR YOURSELF

1. To get the most out of Scripture, we must RECEIVE and TREASURE it. "My son, if you receive my words, and treasure my commands within you . . ." (Proverbs 2:1).

Referring to the Christians in Berea, Acts 17:11 says, "Now the Berean Jews were of more noble character than those in Thessalonica, for they received the message with great eagerness and examined the Scriptures every day to see if what Paul said was true" (NIV). The Bereans checked the accuracy of Paul's teaching against Scripture.

Are you kidding me? They fact-checked *the apostle Paul*?

What a lesson for all of us. If these believers examined the apostle's teaching, then how much more should we be checking out our own pastors, teachers, and so-called modern apostles and prophets?

Some people today claim to speak for God, but if anyone questions the validity of what they say, watch out! They will go ballistic. What foolishness. No one is above being questioned.

Many Christians think they know more than they actually do. Apparently mature believers are often reduced to a blank stare when faced with a question concerning a basic Bible doctrine. They know what they are supposed to believe, but they are unable to defend it biblically. They believe something only because they have been told it is true.

This is very dangerous. We should never hinge our faith merely on what someone has said to us, no matter how credible and godly the source. If that person is saying something that is incorrect, our faith could be shattered. This is why we must base our faith solely on God's Word. We need to know it for ourselves.

The Bible tells us to "be diligent to present yourself approved to God, a worker who does not need to be ashamed, rightly dividing the word of truth" (2 Timothy 2:15). The phrase *rightly dividing* means "dissecting correctly, cutting straight" the word of truth.

Do you believe that Jesus Christ is God?

Do you believe that Jesus Christ is the only way to the Father?

Do you believe that God has a plan for your life and wants to reveal His will for you?

If so, can you open up your Bible and back those beliefs with Scripture? Unfortunately, many Christians can't answer these questions with intelligent, biblical responses.

One reason for this is that often we don't read the Bible with real understanding. Many times when we read, we fail to understand what is being said in its proper context. We have no idea who is speaking or what the circumstances might be surrounding a particular passage.

For instance, reading in the Old Testament about various animal sacrifices could be very confusing if I didn't have a basic understanding of the New Testament. I might conclude that the best way to approach God is to sacrifice an animal. With an understanding of the New Testament, however, I realize that the sacrificial system was foreshadowing what Jesus would do on the cross.

Here are some key questions you might ask yourself as you open the Bible and study a passage of Scripture:

- What is the main subject of the passage?
- Who are the people revealed in this passage?
- Who is speaking?
- About whom is the passage speaking?
- What is the key verse?
- What does it teach me about Jesus?

As you read, it is also very important to ask how the text might apply to your daily living. When reading a passage, ask yourself these questions:

- Is there a sin mentioned that I need to confess or forsake?
- Is there a command given that I should obey?
- Is there a promise made that I can look to in my current circumstances?
- Is there a prayer given that I could pray?

As you read, stop and think about what God may be showing you. It's good to chew your spiritual food. That's what is meant by meditating on Scripture. We are better off reading five verses slowly and understanding what they mean than reading five chapters quickly and not getting anything out of them. Learn to slow down. Learn to allow the Holy Spirit to speak to you through each passage as you read.

2. To get the most out of Bible study, we need to pray for understanding. *"Cry out for insight, and ask for understanding"* (Proverbs 2:3, NLT).

We need to come before the Lord and pray something like, "Father, I believe You are the author of this Book. I believe, as You say in Scripture, that all Scripture is breathed by You. Therefore I am asking You, as the author, to take me on a guided tour. Help me to understand, and show me how these truths apply to my life."

That form of sincere prayer will cause the Bible to come alive in your time of study. The Bible tells us if we want to know God, then we should seek Him and His wisdom as though we were mining for gold or searching for treasures (see Proverbs 2:4).

As believers living in the United States, I doubt that we recognize what a treasure the Bible is to us. We've been spoiled in many ways. Many of us have more than one Bible at home. I own Bibles in different sizes, shapes, and translations.

However, in China (and other countries where the Bible is restricted or even prohibited) it is a treasure. I've heard stories of believers who have had only one Bible for an entire congregation. They take that Bible, tear out pages, and give them to individual members of the congregation to memorize. For many of these Christians, Bibles are as valuable as gold—even more so. We need to see that same value in God's Word and not take it for granted. As Psalm 19:9–10 says, "The laws of the LORD are true; each one is fair. They are more desirable than gold, even the finest gold" (NLT).

Let's say that you somehow misplaced a check worth a thousand dollars. Do you think you would go searching for it? Do you think you would look and look and look until you found it?

There is buried gold in the pages of Scripture. You need to get to it, search for it, and find what is there in the Bible for you.

WHY MEMORIZE?

The best way for me to remember things is to write them down. When I write something down, it becomes engraved more deeply into my memory—much deeper than if I had only read it. I might not even have to refer to what I wrote. Writing something down seems to help the material enter my mind and gives it more staying power. It's a good practice to keep a journal or notebook with your Bible. When you study the Scriptures personally and a passage speaks to you, write down what God has shown you. Maybe it won't be useful right at that moment, but the next day, or even a month later, it may be just what you need.

Once Scripture is ingrained in your memory, it always will be there to use. There will be times when that verse or passage you memorized will pay great dividends. It will bring comfort to your heart, as well as needed strength in a time of intense temptation. The psalmist wrote, "Your word I have hidden in my heart, that I might not sin against You" (Psalm 119:11). Although it's good to carry a Bible in your briefcase, backpack, or purse—or have it available on your smartphone—the best place to carry it is in your heart.

God tells us,

> Fix these words of mine in your hearts and minds; tie them as symbols on your hands and bind them on your foreheads. Teach them to your children, talking about them when you sit at home and when you walk along the road, when you lie down and when you get up. (Deuteronomy 11:18–19, NIV)

Colossians 3:16 says, "Let the word of Christ dwell in you richly." That could be translated, "Let the word of Christ permeate your life," or, "Let the word of Christ be at home inside of you." In other words, let the Bible fill your life. Fall in love with the Word of God. You will never regret it.

APPLYING WHAT WE LEARN

It is not enough to study the Bible on a daily basis or even memorize it; it must affect the way we live. It is not enough to go through the Word of God; the Word of God must go through us. It is not how we mark our Bible; it is how our Bible marks us.

Ultimately we must apply what we learn from the Bible to our everyday actions and activities. Remember, Jesus said that if we abide in His Word, then we are His disciples (see John 8:31). The word *abide* is the same word Jesus used in John 15:7 when He said, "If you abide in Me, and My words abide in you, you will ask what you desire, and it shall be done for you."

We abide in Jesus as we draw strength and resources from Him. In the same way that a vine draws its resources from the soil and the branch draws its resources from the vine, we are to maintain unbroken fellowship, communion, and friendship with God. If we are abiding in God's Word, it means we are drawing our ideas and lifestyle from it. As a result, our actions and speech are being affected.

Is God's Word affecting you today? Is it sustaining your life? Is it controlling your thoughts, the way you conduct your business, your home life, and even your free time? It is only when we put ourselves under the authority of God's Word and submit to its teaching that we become His disciples.

DISCIPLESHIP AND PRAYER

Prayer should be second nature to a Christian, almost like breathing. But sadly, prayer is greatly lacking in the lives of many believers.

A disciple must be a person of prayer. Prayer is one of the essentials of discipleship. It's the key to having passion and power in our witness for Jesus Christ.

When Job encountered his many trials, he cried out, "If only there were someone to mediate between us, someone to bring us together" (Job 9:33, NIV). Job couldn't find anyone to reason or argue for him, to stand in the gap for him before God. He felt as though he couldn't get through to God.

Maybe there have been times when you felt that way too—times when it seemed that the Lord just wasn't listening. But if you have received Jesus Christ as Lord and Savior, this simply shouldn't be the case, because Jesus has opened the way for us to stand boldly at the throne of grace to find help in time of need (see Hebrews 4:16). The Bible tells us that Jesus lives to make intercession for us (see Hebrews 7:25).

Today we can approach God through Jesus, our Mediator: "For there is one God and one mediator between God and mankind, the man Christ Jesus" (1 Timothy 2:5, NIV).

The great, indescribable value of prayer is that it keeps us in touch with God. God wants you to get to know Him through prayer. He wants to reveal Himself to you through prayer.

We might expect God to give us all that we need for every situation all at once, in one big package. But that is not the way it works. In fact, that would be dangerous.

God has a lot to give us, but He gives it to us *as we need it*. Prayer brings us into dependence on God as He works in our lives.

In Matthew 6, we find Jesus dealing with several common misconceptions people have regarding prayer. The first misconception concerned motives. Jesus said, "And when you pray, do not be like the hypocrites, for they love to pray standing in the synagogues and on the street corners to be seen by others. Truly I tell you, they have received their reward in full" (verse 5, NIV).

The problem with the religious people of that day, the Pharisees, was that they prayed to impress others. They could be seen on street corners and in the marketplace lifting up their hands and praying in a very attention-getting manner. (If there had been TV cameras in those days, these guys would have known how to get in front of one.) Others would walk by and think, *Wow, just look at that man of God. He loves God so much that he can't even wait to get to the synagogue to pray!*

What they didn't realize was that the person praying was most likely thinking, *What a man of God I am! Everyone is*

*looking at me. Everyone is impressed with my spirituality. I am
so holy.*

That type of attitude will result in a prayer left unheard
by God. A person so concerned with what others are thinking about him is too full of himself to be effective in his
prayer. Make no mistake — spiritual pride is as much a sin as
lying or immorality, even though it is a more subtle one.

The next misconception Jesus addressed was *how* the
Pharisees were praying: "And when you pray, do not keep on
babbling like pagans, for they think they will be heard
because of their many words" (verse 7, NIV). The Pharisees
were caught up in repeating ritualized prayers over and over
again. They seemed to believe that the longer the prayer, the
more spiritual and pleasing to God.

But God isn't interested in eloquence. *Not at all.*

Prayer should come from the heart. He isn't interested in
how perfectly our prayers sound, or whether they rhyme, or
whether we throw in any King James English, or how long
they are. He is concerned with how genuine they are. One of
the most eloquent prayers found in Scripture comes from a
man who said, "God, be merciful to me a sinner!" (Luke
18:13). Now that is an effective prayer. That is a man who
was honest with God. He said what he was thinking and
simply laid it out before the Lord.

And guess what? Jesus Himself said that man's prayer
was *heard.*

Sometimes we get so concerned with technique that we
completely miss the whole point of prayer. The word *pray*
that Jesus used literally means "to wish forward." "Wish"
describes a desire, a hope of our heart. "Forward" implies
action. It is the idea of wishing something from the depth of

the heart and bringing that desire forward to the throne of God. Often our mouths and minds can go through some ritualized prayer, while our hearts never engage at all.

Sometimes people wonder what the best posture for prayer is. Is it on your knees? Is it okay to pray with your eyes open? Sure it is. It doesn't cancel out your prayer if your eyes are open. But I think it's a good thing to close your eyes when you pray, because it helps you to concentrate. You can pray on your knees, or you can pray sitting down or lying down. You can even pray while you're driving (if you remember to keep your eyes open). Many people enjoy taking a long walk with the Lord, praying as they keep their legs moving.

The Bible tells us that people prayed in all sorts of unusual places. They prayed in prison. They prayed on mountaintops. They prayed in valleys. One man even prayed from the belly of a great fish, and God heard his prayer. Wherever you are, you can pray.

Another common misconception Jesus unmasked was the true purpose of prayer. He said, "Your Father knows what you need before you ask him" (verse 8, NIV). God knows our needs before we ask. Prayer, then, isn't instructing or informing God. Nor is it bending the will of God. Some people think they can influence God or move God a certain way through prayer. But nothing could be further from the truth. True prayer isn't overcoming or changing God's reluctance; it's laying hold of His willingness. Prayer isn't getting our will in heaven; it's getting God's will on earth. Martin Luther said, "By our praying . . . we are instructing ourselves more than Him."[1]

"TEACH US TO PRAY"

"Lord, teach us to pray. . . ."

That was the request one of the disciples brought before Jesus (see Luke 11:1). No doubt it was because the disciples had watched Jesus in prayer. Sometimes Jesus would stay up all night in the presence of His Heavenly Father and pray. While the disciples would be sleeping, Jesus would be praying. In the Garden of Gethsemane, shortly before His arrest, Jesus told Peter, "Watch and pray, lest you enter into temptation. The spirit indeed is willing, but the flesh is weak" (Matthew 26:41).

In response to the disciple's request, Jesus gave us a template for prayer that we call the Lord's Prayer. A more accurate name for it would be the Disciples' Prayer, because it is for us to pray—not Him. Jesus never needed to pray, "And forgive us our debts, as we forgive our debtors" (Matthew 6:12). He was sinless. This was a prayer for His disciples and for us.

Within this prayer, we are given the principles we need to understand how to communicate with God. The disciples had watched Jesus pray. They had seen Him spend time with His Father. They had seen His intimacy and His closeness with the Father. In contrast, they had also seen the ritualized, cold, academic prayers of the religious hypocrites.

So Jesus began His lesson on prayer by saying, "In this manner, therefore, pray . . ." (Matthew 6:9). Another translation says, "Pray along these lines . . ." (TLB).

In other words, Jesus wasn't giving the disciples a canned, formalized prayer here. In fact, this prayer was never repeated in the New Testament—not even once. That isn't to say that it is wrong to pray this prayer verbatim or to use it as an act of worship to God.

But Jesus never intended for it to be a ritual.

There is nothing magical about saying it, and it doesn't get God's attention any more than any other prayer from one of His kids. We can, however, learn from its form and structure how to pray more effectively. It is a model and pattern for all prayers.

This prayer is divided into two sections. The first three petitions focus on the glory of God, while the last three deal with our need as humans.

It should be pointed out that the prayer begins with "Our Father in heaven" and not with "Give us this day our daily bread." Too often, we begin our prayers with our needs.

"OUR FATHER IN HEAVEN"

When we pray, we should first recognize the One we are speaking to: *"Our Father in heaven"* (Matthew 6:9). It is good to pause before you speak in prayer, realizing that you are addressing the Creator of the universe. Too often we rush into the presence of God and absentmindedly rattle off our petitions. We ought to first be quiet and wait before the Lord before saying anything. Then, after a time of contemplation of whom we are addressing, we will more reverently pray, "Our Father . . ."

To whom are we speaking? We aren't throwing random, empty words into the wind. We are speaking to our God and Father—the One who loves us, sent His own Son to die for us, and always has our best interests at heart.

As 1 John 3:1 reminds us, "Behold what manner of love the Father has bestowed on us, that we should be called children of God!" From this we can be assured that whatever happens as a result, our prayer is in accordance with what our Father wants for us. Does that mean we will always (with our limited knowledge and finite perspective) understand or agree with everything He does in our lives?

Of course not.

But we can be assured that His will for us is *good*. We know He loves us with an everlasting love.

When you have been around a little while, you begin to have the advantage of twenty-twenty hindsight. You can look back on your life and see how God's wisdom has prevailed. I can think of things for which I prayed years ago, things I was certain were the will of God for me, and He said no. Some of those prayers were answered some time later. And some of them never were answered in the way that I prayed them. But now I can look back and say, "Lord, thank You for the way that You worked in my life."

You need to trust that your Father in heaven is doing the same for you right now. Psalm 84:11 says, "No good thing will He withhold from those who walk uprightly." Just because God is saying no doesn't mean that He has somehow lost your file or that He is turning His back on you. It means that He is looking out for your welfare.

"HALLOWED BE YOUR NAME"

Once we have found our focus and taken time to realize whom we are speaking to, we are then reminded of His holiness: *"Hallowed be Your name"* (Matthew 6:9). The word *hallowed* also could be translated "sanctified," "revered," or "holy."

Another translation says it like this: "May your name be kept holy" (NLT).

How good and right it is to honor God's name, to keep it holy! In our world and in our culture, we hear His name dishonored, mocked, misrepresented, and dragged through the mud every day. But it's different for us, isn't it? We are His own children—His sons and daughters. We have the opportunity to honor, lift high, and speak rightly of His great name and the perfection of His character.

Saying "hallowed be Your name" recognizes that we should want to be sanctified, or set apart, for Jesus Christ to live holy lives. Because He is holy, so we also should live holy lives. All of our ambitions, interests, and pursuits should reveal that we follow a holy God.

The privilege of prayer wasn't given to us so that we could demand things from God. James 4:3 tells us why some of our prayers go unanswered: "When you ask, you do not receive, because you ask with wrong motives, that you may spend what you get on your pleasures" (NIV). We should ask for the things God wants to give us. If He gave us everything we asked for, it ultimately would destroy us. We must seek His glory more than our own desires.

I have found that when I seek God's glory, His will, and His kingdom, He blesses me. It is not wrong to ask for what you believe is necessary, but I make it a point to begin my prayers with something like, "Lord, I think this would be a great thing for You to do, and I really think You ought to do it, but Your will be done. If I'm missing something, if there's more to this than I know, then overrule me here. I know that whatever You do will be best." That is praying with His glory in mind.

"YOUR KINGDOM COME"

The next phrase in our model prayer is *"Your kingdom come. Your will be done on earth as it is in heaven"* (verse 10). A person can't really pray, "Your kingdom come," until he or she can first pray, "My kingdom go."

All too often, our prayers are meant to establish our own interests, our own kingdom. We want to be the captain of our own ship, the master of our own destiny. This won't do if we truly want His kingdom and if we truly want to be His disciples. We must turn over the reins of leadership completely to Him.

For this reason, it is essential that we learn what the will of God is so that we can pray for it. If you pray according to the will of God, your prayers always will be answered with a yes. According to 1 John 5:14–15, "Now this is the confidence that we have in Him, that if we ask anything according to His will, He hears us. And if we know that He hears us, whatever we ask, we know that we have the petitions that we have asked of Him."

As we spend time in the Word of God as a disciple, learning the will of God and the desires of God, our prayers will change. They no longer will be self-centered or self-indulgent. Instead, they will be oriented toward the glory and will of God. As we align ourselves with His will and start praying for it, we will begin to see the results. Most prayers are not answered because they are outside the will of God.

Once we have discovered God's will, we can then pray aggressively and confidently for it. We can pray, believing it will happen, because we know it is not something we have dreamed up.

When Jesus went to His hometown, we are told that "He

did not do many mighty works there because of their unbelief'" (Matthew 13:58). In other words, unbelief will cancel our own prayers. We must pray, believing.

So where do we get such faith? "Faith comes by hearing, and hearing by the word of God" (Romans 10:17). I can pray, believing that God will save a person's soul, because I am told in Scripture that God is "not willing that any should perish but that all should come to repentance" (2 Peter 3:9). I can pray, then, believing and hoping that God will save that individual. Nevertheless, the ultimate result is God's doing and not my praying.

I can also pray with biblical authority for revival in our country, city, home, or church. I believe this is something God wants to do, because as we have seen, it is clearly proclaimed in Scripture (see 2 Chronicles 7:14). And on a more personal level, I can pray authoritatively that God would make me more like Jesus and that He would reveal His will to me (see Romans 8:29; 12:2). Scripture speaks clearly of many things we can know *for sure* are God's will.

"GIVE US THIS DAY OUR DAILY BREAD"

After establishing whom we are speaking to and acknowledging His rightful position, we then come to the first petition: *"Give us this day our daily bread"* (Matthew 6:11).

Let me again emphasize the order of Jesus' model prayer. Before a word of personal petition is uttered, Jesus shows us that we must first realize who it is we are speaking to and ask for His will above our own. God is our heavenly Father, not our heavenly butler or some personal genie.

Also notice that Jesus doesn't say, "Give us this *year* our *yearly* bread," or even, "Give us this *month* our *monthly* bread." God wants us to rely on Him *daily.* Sadly, many people don't want to depend on God; they would rather depend on themselves.

It is noteworthy that in John 6, Jesus described Himself as the Bread of Life. We must seek a fresh encounter each day with Him. Yesterday's "bread" is largely useless for today, much like the manna provided by God for the children of Israel during their wilderness wanderings. The manna would not keep overnight without spoiling; it was good for that day only.

The same applies to your spiritual lives. God wants to give you fresh direction each day. Scripture tells us, "Because of the LORD's great love we are not consumed, for his compassions never fail. They are new every morning; great is your faithfulness" (Lamentations 3:22–23, NIV). God wants to bring newness into your relationship with Him.

"FORGIVE US OUR DEBTS"

In Matthew 6:12, we read, *"And forgive us our debts, as we forgive our debtors."* A true disciple will recognize the need for confession of sin, because the Bible says that unconfessed sin will hinder prayer (see Psalm 66:18). If we hold on to or cling to sin in our lives, God simply won't hear us. We should always remember to ask God to forgive our sins, even those we aren't immediately aware of. After all, the only sin God cannot forgive is the one we won't confess.

Some people have misunderstood the second part of the phrase "as we forgive our debtors." They teach that the condition of being forgiven is that we must first forgive others. I don't believe this, because it is a clear contradiction of other scriptural teachings. The only basis for receiving forgiveness from God is asking for it: "If we confess our sins, He is faithful and just to forgive us our sins and to cleanse us from all unrighteousness" (1 John 1:9).

Clearly God doesn't make forgiving others a prerequisite for being forgiven. What He is saying is this: "If you have really been forgiven and understand something of that forgiveness, then you will be forgiving of other people." If you are not forgiving of others, then I question whether you know anything of God's forgiveness in your own life.

A forgiven person will be a forgiving person. A true disciple will harbor no grudge toward another. The disciple knows it will hinder his or her prayer life and walk with God.

For that reason, no child of God can walk around with bitterness, anger, or hostility in his heart toward another person without feeling the conviction of his sin. We must forgive others as we have been forgiven.

"DO NOT LEAD US INTO TEMPTATION"

Jesus concludes this prayer with, *"And do not lead us into temptation, but deliver us from the evil one. For Yours is the kingdom and the power and the glory forever. Amen"* (Matthew 6:13). The "evil one" is an obvious reference to Satan. We are to recognize our total weakness apart from God and the fact that we are engaged in a spiritual battle. We need our Father's protection. Without Him, we are completely vulnerable. We must depend on Him for daily bread, depend on His will for direction, and depend on Him for power.

ACTS

Another way to remember the structure of this model prayer is to use the acronym ACTS:

Adoration
Confession
Thanksgiving
Supplication

First, I adore God and praise Him. Then I confess my sin. Next I remember to give thanks. Then I offer my supplications, or requests.

With this model prayer as our guide, you and I can be in an attitude of prayer — and have a running conversation with our Lord — all day long. We will, as the apostle Paul said in 1 Thessalonians 5:17, "pray without ceasing."

A big part of being a disciple is simply enjoying the nearness and presence of the God who loves us.

DISCIPLESHIP
AND THE CHURCH

So far, we have looked at two essentials for our growth as disciples of Jesus Christ: Bible study and prayer. The third essential involves the significance of the church in the life of the disciple.

I can't stress this enough. I can't begin to express how important it is for a believer to be plugged in to a local fellowship of believers. As we come into the church and find our place in it, we are then in a position to give to others what God has given us. Every Christian has an important role in the body of Christ, and God has given special gifts to each one.

The emphasis, however, isn't only on what a believer gets from the church, but on what he or she can contribute. The Bible tells us to "think of ways to motivate one another to acts of love and good works. And let us not neglect our meeting together, as some people do, but encourage one another, especially now that the day of his return is drawing near" (Hebrews 10:24–25, NLT).

The church isn't only a place where we can be taught God's Word and worship Him; it's also a place where we can come to be equipped for service.

A healthy church will be filled with believers who desire not only to receive, but to give. Rather than having an attitude that says, "Bless me; do something for me," they will want to help out. They want to follow the example of Jesus, who came not to be served but to serve (see Matthew 20:28; Mark 10:45).

The number-one priority in selecting a church should not be how close it is to your home or how nice its facilities are. The most important thing is to ask, "Is this church teaching God's Word?" People should bring their Bibles to church and read from them in the service. The pastor should preach from the Bible as well.

But as we take in, we should also recognize our privilege and responsibility to give out. Yes, we truly do need to receive when we walk through the doors of the church. We need to be encouraged, taught, and nourished in our spirit. But in the process, we might discover something very interesting: The more we *give*, the more capacity we will find in ourselves to receive what God has for us.

If a need or opportunity arises, we should be willing to leave our nice, comfortable seat and volunteer. The right attitude of a truly thankful Christian is "God has given to me and, as a result, I want to give to others."

THE FUNCTION OF SPIRITUAL GIFTS

God has given gifts to each of us who have put our faith in Jesus Christ, and He has empowered us with the Holy Spirit.

Are you using and cultivating the gifts God has given you? The Bible specifically tells us that as believers, we are to use our spiritual gifts as we await the return of Christ (see 1 Corinthians 1:7).

Also, failing to discover and use the gifts God has given us could cause us to quench the Holy Spirit, which the Bible specifically commands us not to do (see 1 Thessalonians 5:19). *Quench* carries the idea of extinguishing something. So when God's Spirit nudges us to say or do a certain thing and we refuse, we are quenching the Spirit.

Some Christians feel adverse toward the gifts of the Spirit, probably because there has been so much abuse in this area. Often those who claim to be using the gifts of the Spirit are some of the strangest people around. As a result, we conclude that if these are the gifts of the Holy Spirit, then we don't want anything to do with them.

But let's not look at the gifts that way. Let's take a step back and look at them in a biblical and balanced way. I believe in the power of the Holy Spirit, but I believe it is a *practical* power that God wants us to have in our lives, the same power that caused the early church to turn their world upside down.

Ephesians 4, a definitive chapter on the gifts of the Spirit, explains why God has given them: "And He Himself gave some to be apostles, some prophets, some evangelists, and some pastors and teachers, *for the equipping of the saints for the work of ministry, for the edifying of the body of Christ*" (verses 11–12, emphasis added).

First, we see that God has given the gifts of the Spirit for the perfecting, or the maturing, of the saints. God has raised up pastor-teachers, evangelists, and prophets to help us grow up:

> So that we should no longer be children, tossed to
> and fro and carried about with every wind of doc-
> trine, by the trickery of men, in the cunning
> craftiness of deceitful plotting, but, speaking the
> truth in love, may grow up in all things into Him
> who is the head—Christ. (verses 14-15)

God gives us these gifts, working through people like pastor-teachers, so we will be equipped and mature.

Second, God has given the gifts of the Spirit so we will be equipped to do all God has called us to do in the church. God has a gift, or gifts, for you to use to bless others. The gifts of the Spirit aren't a hobby to play with; they are tools to build with and weapons to fight with.

Third, God has given the gifts of the Spirit to bring unity in the church, "till we all come to the unity of the faith and of the knowledge of the Son of God, to a perfect man, to the measure of the stature of the fullness of Christ" (verse 13). As we use these gifts, we discover that no one person has all the gifts. God, in His sovereign will, has chosen to give certain gifts to certain people. As Romans 12:4–6 reminds us,

> Just as each of us has one body with many mem-
> bers, and these members do not all have the same
> function, so in Christ we, though many, form one
> body, and each member belongs to all the others.
> We have different gifts, according to the grace
> given to each of us. (NIV)

Fourth, God has given the gifts of the Spirit for the *spiritual* growth of Christians and for the numerical growth of the church: "From him the whole body, joined and held together by every supporting ligament, grows and builds itself up in love, as each part does its work" (Ephesians 4:16, NIV). When a church is grounded in God's Word and energized by the Holy Spirit, it will reach out, not satisfied to stay to itself. It will permeate, challenge, and confront our culture.

It is power with a purpose!

SECRETS OF THE EARLY CHURCH

If God kept a baby book of the church, He would certainly have a page devoted to the events described in Acts 2, the church's first day. To better understand how we should function as disciples, we need to look at the New Testament church as Jesus established it. In Acts 2, we find the first-century disciples in action. We also find principles that make for an effective church and for the true disciple's place in it.

At first glance, this text reveals that the early church was dramatically different from much of the church today. What was normal to them is radical to us. Discipleship is really radical Christian living. Normal Christian living as presented in the New Testament was a passionate, Spirit-empowered, all-consuming devotion to God and to His Word.

We must always remember that the early church was set in motion by the Holy Spirit. To be effective Christians, we must also depend on the power of the Holy Spirit. There is a dimension of power available for every believer beyond the conversion experience. When we become Christians, the Holy Spirit takes up residence inside of us. He is there to guide us into all truth. He is there to seal us with His assurance that we are children of God.

But there is yet another dimension of power available to us as believers. Jesus said to His disciples, "You shall receive power when the Holy Spirit has come upon you; and you shall be witnesses to Me in Jerusalem, and in all Judea and Samaria, and to the end of the earth" (Acts 1:8). The word Jesus used for *upon* is different from words used elsewhere when speaking of the Spirit coming inside of us. This experience is an empowering one that gives us the boldness we need to live the Christian life. It is the power to live a consistent life, the power to be bold enough to share your faith.

The early church began in the power of the Holy Spirit and continued that way. If we want to flourish and be effective in our witness for Jesus Christ, then we must begin in the power of the Spirit *and stay dependent upon that power until our last day.*

"THEY CONTINUED STEADFASTLY"

In Acts 2:42, we find the first key to the early disciples' effectiveness: "They continued steadfastly in the apostles' doctrine and fellowship, in the breaking of bread, and in prayers."

The early Christians had an intense passion to participate in the life of the church. Not only was there passion behind their actions, but there was a consistency, a steadfastness about them. Passion and consistency were the keys to helping them do God's will.

And there's one other thing that jumps out at us from this portrait of the early believers. They didn't take the privilege of meeting together for granted. The more I travel, the more thankful I have become for what God is doing here in our country, in our own churches. Pastors in Eastern Europe have told me how hard it is to do what God wants them to do with the restrictions imposed by government. Pastors in Ethiopia have told me how they and members of their congregations have been tortured and imprisoned for preaching the gospel and following Jesus. We are privileged here in the United States to have the freedoms we do. We must never take them for granted, and we must remember to pray for our brothers and sisters who live in countries where religious freedom is not tolerated.

The early believers' passion was directed toward fellowship. We have somehow lost the true meaning of the word *fellowship*. Often we hear it used at church gatherings, where there promises to be "food, fun, and fellowship." But is that what the early church was experiencing? Quick hellos and goodbyes? Shallow conversations about football scores and the weather? Doughnuts and coffee? What is fellowship, exactly?

First of all, authentic fellowship isn't just Christian social activity. Though it may involve that to some extent, true fellowship encompasses a much greater commitment. The word used for fellowship in the New Testament is a very distinct Greek word: *koinonia*. It also can be translated "communion," "partnership," "contribution," and "distribution." Each of these words provides a different facet of *koinonia*.

In part, fellowship is a common link with another individual that includes friendship, spiritual intimacy, unity, and a partnership in doing the work of Christ here on earth.

The word *communion* speaks of friendship and intimacy. God wants us to have friendship and intimacy not only with Him, but with one another. It's a bond that can bring Christians together like no other bond, even closer than the bond of a family. You could meet a believer on the other side of the world, and even though you don't share the same culture or language, you could find yourself experiencing a deeper connection than you possess with your next-door neighbor, who might share a hundred surface-level things in common with you. Two believers share a unique exchange as God's Spirit works in their lives.

Then there is the word *partnership,* which implies cooperation. Fellowship isn't just some mystical communion; it's also practical. It involves helping and working with another person, as well as praying for and worshiping with that individual.

Next, there are the elements of contribution and distribution. These also imply practical help for fellow believers through the sharing of food, clothing, and other needs. The Bible tells us that if we see brothers and sisters destitute and in need and fail to help them, then we are without faith (see James 2:15–17). When confronted with such a situation, we need to obey God and help our fellow Christians. That is fellowship. We see this element of fellowship clearly at work in the early church as we read that they shared "all things in common" (Acts 2:44).

God delights in His people gathering together for *koinonia.* In fact, God promised to show Himself in unique ways at these times. The psalmist wrote that God inhabits the praises of Israel (see Psalm 22:3). When we, with other believers, set our eyes and hearts above our circumstances and focus on our Father, it brings everything into perspective. What's best is that we experience God's presence in unique ways at those times.

Along with fellowship, the early Christians also "continued . . . in prayers" (Acts 2:42). The word *prayer* also could be translated "steadfast earnestness." As I pointed out in the last chapter, prayer is a key element in being a disciple of Jesus. But it is also a primary element of an effective church. The early church was characterized by steadfast, earnest prayer.

GLADNESS AND SIMPLICITY OF HEART

The first-century disciples had "gladness and simplicity of heart" (Acts 2:46). Are you glad when it is time to go to church? David wrote, "I was glad when they said to me, 'Let us go into the house of the LORD'" (Psalm 122:1). These days, some people could say, "I was *mad* when they said to me, 'Let us go into the house of the LORD'"!

The early church focused on what was important, and they let nothing get in the way. If we allow ourselves to be consistently influenced by the things of this world, it will dull our appetite for God's Word and will pull us away from Him. It also will lessen our interest in prayer and our desire to be with God's people.

But when we are living as disciples, we will look forward to going to church on a consistent and frequent basis. Meeting with other believers will be like a spiritual oasis where we can be refreshed. It will be an occasion to encourage one another as we go out to live in this world as witnesses for Jesus Christ.

Finally, we read, "The Lord added to the church daily those who were being saved" (Acts 2:47). A healthy church is a growing church. Likewise, a healthy believer is one who will be a shining light in this world of darkness. Even as the Lord adds to the church daily, a disciple of Jesus will be an instrument of God, drawing people to Christ by doing his or her part within the church.

OUR FUTURE REWARD

One day, you will stand before God, and He will reward you for your faithfulness to Him. He will not overlook even the smallest, seemingly most insignificant gesture on behalf of the kingdom of God. Jesus said that in our service to God, even if it is never seen by other human eyes, it is seen by Him: "Your Father who sees in secret will Himself reward you openly" (Matthew 6:4).

Speaking of this day in the future, the Bible says, "We must all appear before the judgment seat of Christ, so that each of us may receive what is due us for the things done while in the body, whether good or bad" (2 Corinthians 5:10, NIV).

This isn't to be confused with the Great White Throne Judgment (see Revelation 20), where anyone not found written in the Book of Life is cast into the lake of fire. This Great White Throne Judgment is only for the nonbeliever.

We find more about the judgment seat of Christ (the Bema Seat Judgment), exclusively for believers, in 1 Corinthians 3:

> For no one can lay any foundation other than the one we already have—Jesus Christ. Anyone who builds on that foundation may use a variety of materials—gold, silver, jewels, wood, hay, or straw. But on the judgment day, fire will reveal what kind of work each builder has done. The fire will show if a person's work has any value. If the work survives, that builder will receive a reward. (verses 11-14, NLT)

According to this and other passages, our *presence* in the kingdom is guaranteed by the promises of God, but our *position* in the kingdom will be won or lost by the quality of service we render here and now. Salvation is a gift to us because we have put our faith in Jesus; honor is a reward for service to Jesus. It's about receiving rewards for what you have done for God. The wood, hay, or straw represents squandered resources, time, and indeed, an entire life.

There is nothing wrong with having a career. But if that career was more important in your life than God, then you will have a problem. If possessions were more important than God, or a hobby, or even a ministry, then at the judgment seat of Christ, the fire will go through those things and nothing will be left to show for your life.

One day, God will want to know what you did with the gifts and talents He has given you. Every one of us has been given certain skills and talents. You have something to bring in the service of God.

Yet many times we don't use our gifts for His glory. Instead, we chase after what we want in life. The Bible teaches that we are put on this earth to bring glory to God. That is why we are here. God says, "Everyone who is called by My name, whom I have created for My glory; I have formed him, yes, I have made him" (Isaiah 43:7).

Let's mark it well in our minds and hearts: We are to glorify Him in all that we do with our lives.

DISCIPLING OTHERS

This is the most important chapter in this book. This is what I have been building toward, for we now come to the practical result of being a disciple of Jesus Christ: passing on what we have learned and discipling others.

Prior to Jesus' ascending into heaven, He gave His disciples these marching orders:

> "All authority has been given to Me in heaven and on earth. Go therefore and make disciples of all the nations, baptizing them in the name of the Father and of the Son and of the Holy Spirit, teaching them to observe all things that I have commanded you; and lo, I am with you always, even to the end of the age." (Matthew 28:18-20)

To feel the impact these orders are to have on our lives as His disciples, we must make two important observations.

First, the three verses you just read are often referred to

as the Great Commission. Notice that it's a *commission* as opposed to a *suggestion.* Jesus didn't suggest that we might carry the gospel to the world if we had time and felt like it. Rather, He *commanded* it. And that same command holds true in our day too.

Second, these words weren't directed only to the original twelve disciples, nor are they meant exclusively for pastors, evangelists, and missionaries. They are for every follower and disciple of Jesus Christ. If I am His disciple, then I am commanded to go and make disciples of others. And if I am not making disciples of others, then I am not really being the disciple He wants me to be.

What, then, does it mean to make disciples? Verse 20 defines it as "teaching them to observe all things that I have commanded you." Simply put, it is not only sharing our faith with others, but it is also living out our faith so that people have the opportunity to observe it in action.

With this understanding, we now have a proper basis for examining in greater detail what it means to disciple another individual.

EMPOWERED FOR THE TASK

God never will ask us to do anything that He won't empower us to accomplish. The calling of God is the enabling of God (see 2 Corinthians 3:4–6). If He has commanded us to go and make disciples, then we can be confident He will be there to give us the ability to see it through.

Notice Jesus said, "All authority has been given to Me in heaven and on earth. Go therefore and make disciples." From this we see that if the power is in Jesus Christ and He is living inside of us, then His power and resources are at our disposal to accomplish the task.

When we reach for courage, it will be there.

When we reach for power, it will be there.

When we reach for wisdom, it will be there.

And we all need to ask God for a strong daily dose of boldness from the Holy Spirit. In Acts 4:23–31, we see an interesting display of this boldness in the lives of Peter and John. As I pointed out in chapter 2, they had been preaching the gospel, which infuriated the religious leaders. As a result, they were arrested and forbidden to ever preach again. They couldn't comply with that, however, so they prayed,

> "Now, Lord, look on their threats, and grant to Your servants that with all boldness they may speak Your word, by stretching out Your hand to heal, and that signs and wonders may be done through the name of Your holy Servant Jesus." (verses 29–30)

After they prayed, the Bible tells us the place where they were meeting was shaken, and they were filled with the Holy Spirit and spoke the word of God boldly.

Here Peter and John were in trouble for their outspokenness, so what did they do? *They prayed for even greater boldness.* They had laid hold of Jesus' promise to them in Acts 1:8: "You shall receive power when the Holy Spirit has come upon you; and you shall be witnesses to Me . . ."

Most of us suddenly become chickenhearted when it comes to sharing the gospel. We need to ask God for the power He has made available to us.

The hardest thing about sharing your faith with

nonbelievers is getting started, forcing those first words out of your mouth. That is where the power of the Holy Spirit is essential. Then once the ball is rolling, you will discover that sharing your faith can become a joy as well as a great blessing. Better yet, you may play an important role in changing someone's eternal destiny.

THE SALT OF THE EARTH

Jesus concluded His own definition of discipleship in the Gospel of Luke by saying, "Salt is good; but if the salt has lost its flavor, how shall it be seasoned?" (Luke 14:34).

To receive the full benefit of what Jesus was saying, we need to understand the first-century mindset. In Roman culture, salt was very important. Next to the sun, salt was the most important thing there was. Often Roman soldiers were actually paid in salt, which is where the expression "He's not worth his salt" originates. With this in mind, Jesus is saying, "You are to be salt in this earth. You are valuable. You can make a difference."

A distinct quality of salt is that it affects everything it comes into contact with. For instance, just a little pinch of salt in a glass of water can be tasted. In the same way, even one faithful Christian in an ungodly situation or place can make a difference.

Salt also stimulates thirst. When you buy popcorn at the movie theater, you quickly discover that it has been heavily salted, probably with the intent of stimulating your thirst so you'll traipse back to the lobby to buy one of those massive sodas they sell.

In the same way, if we live godly lives, it can stimulate

spiritual thirst in the lives of others. (This really works!) If unbelievers see something different in you, if they see that you aren't like everyone else and that you live a life directed by certain spiritual principles, they can find it very appealing. Many unbelievers are also influenced when they see a Christian face severe circumstances and still maintain a sense of calmness and peace. Our lives are the only Bible many people ever will read. Christians are to be living letters from the hand of God Himself and read by people everywhere we go (see 2 Corinthians 3:2).

One of the greatest compliments paid to a Christian is when a nonbeliever says, "What's different about you? There's a quality that I admire, and I want to know more. Tell me about what you believe." That is being salt.

On the other hand, smacking nonbelievers across the head with a Bible is not being a witness for Jesus. A more effective witness would be to let those nonbelievers around you watch and see the difference God has made in your life. Even something as subtle as taking your Bible to work and reading it quietly during lunch or on your break could have a great impact.

Jesus has called us to be fishers of men, and one thing that is helpful in fulfilling that role is to first throw out the bait. If I want to start a conversation with the person next to me on a plane, I often pull out my Bible and set it on the tray. Some people look at me as though I have a highly contagious disease, and they want to quickly move. But there are others who will ask what I am reading. This often opens the door to share God's truth.

When you want to share your faith with someone, it's generally a good idea to first talk about how God is working in your own life. Give people an opportunity, and if they respond, reel them in a bit by telling them a little more about Jesus. If their interest continues to grow, you can then explain what it means to know Christ, what Christ did, and what our response should be to Him.

Sometimes the conversation will come to a point where someone doesn't want to hear any more. If that is the case, don't push it. As 2 Timothy 2:24–25 says,

> The Lord's servant must not be quarrelsome but must be kind to everyone, able to teach, not resentful. Opponents must be gently instructed, in the hope that God will grant them repentance leading them to a knowledge of the truth. (NIV)

You can come to a point where a person has heard enough. That is the time to simply pull back and say, "If you want to know more, just read the Bible, and I'll pray for you." I often recommend reading the Gospel of John, because it was written so that we may believe that Jesus was the Son of God (see John 20:31). In the future, maybe that person who was once resistant will start the conversation again.

Our responsibility as Christians is simply to proclaim the truth of the gospel and leave the conversion process to God.

THE LIGHT OF THE WORLD

Jesus used two analogies to show the impact Christians should have in this world: salt and light. We've already seen what salt does. In contrast to being salt, which is primarily living what you believe, light signifies *proclaiming* what you believe.

Jesus said, "Let your light so shine before men, that they may see your good works and glorify your Father in heaven" (Matthew 5:16). Too many believers try to be light without first being salt. They talk the Christian talk, but they don't walk the Christian walk. Quite honestly, it would be better if they didn't say a thing if they are unable to back it up with their lifestyle.

In contrast, there are those who are salt without being light. They live godly lives, but they don't tell people why. We must find the balance. Romans 10:14 says, "But how can they call on him to save them unless they believe in him? And how can they believe in him if they have never heard about him? And how can they hear about him unless someone tells them?" (NLT). God wants us to be instruments through which He can speak.

There is a right way and a wrong way to share the gospel message. That is why it's so important to rely on Jesus and let Him guide us. I believe that God wants us to be sharpshooters, not machine gunners. I have seen machine-gun evangelists who gauge their success by how many people they can talk to in one hour. If you are doing that instead of really taking time with someone, then it may not have any real or lasting effect. It may even drive people away.

I have found that the most effective sharing takes time. It is far better to sit down for an hour and talk genuinely with one person than to rattle off trite clichés to scores of people. Some of the most profound things Jesus ever said were in one-on-one conversations. His talks with the Samaritan woman (see John 4:5–42) and with Nicodemus (see John 3:1–21) have become our scripts for evangelism. Jesus took time for these individuals, so how much more should we take time for those with whom we are speaking?

We need to learn to let God's Holy Spirit lead as we share our faith. When a person comes to Christ, it will be a result of God's work, not our own. Jesus said, "No one can come to Me unless it has been granted to him by My Father" (John 6:65). You might as well know right up front that *no brilliant argument will ever win over another person*. It must be the work of the Holy Spirit, and it must be in God's timing. Scripture tells us, "Be prepared, whether the time is favorable or not" (2 Timothy 4:2, NLT). We need to always be ready, because we never know when we will be called into action.

A STATE OF READINESS

Think of Philip, whom God simply told to go to the desert (see Acts 8:26–40).

He didn't tell Philip why.

He didn't tell Philip for how long.

He didn't tell him there would be a wealthy and powerful man from Ethiopia who would be searching for God and waiting for him when he arrived. He just told him to go to the desert. Philip obeyed, and upon his arrival, he found the man. His timing was just right. If Philip had lagged behind or run ahead, he would have missed out on the opportunity to lead this man to Christ.

Often we miss out on opportunities that God brings our way simply because we're distracted, spiritually asleep, and just not paying attention. Undoubtedly, God can get the job done without us. He will find someone else, but we will miss out on the privilege of being used by Him.

We can also learn a great deal from Philip's methods. He

asked this Ethiopian an interesting question when he heard him reading from the writings of the prophet Isaiah: "Do you understand what you are reading?" (verse 30). The Ethiopian responded by saying, "How can I, unless someone guides me?" (verse 31).

DO WE CARE ENOUGH TO SHARE?

Do you share your faith with others on a regular basis? If not, why not? If most Christians today were brutally honest, many of us would have to admit that we really don't care about the plight of the nonbeliever.

Evangelism must start with a genuine concern for the lost. The people we talk to can tell when we're sincere. Paul had such a concern. He was so stirred for his own people to come to Christ that he said, "My heart is filled with bitter sorrow and unending grief for my people, my Jewish brothers and sisters. I would be willing to be forever cursed—cut off from Christ!—if that would save them" (Romans 9:2–3, NLT).

Moses had the same heart for Israel. We read in Exodus 32 that Moses went to Mount Sinai to receive the commandments of God. But when days passed and Moses hadn't returned to the camp, the people grew desperate and looked for a replacement for God in their lives. Under the misdirected leadership of Aaron, a golden calf was made and the people began to worship it.

As the sinful activity of the people was unfolding, God told Moses, "Go, get down! For your people whom you brought out of the land of Egypt have corrupted themselves" (verse 7).

God went on to speak about the guilt of the people, and Moses interrupted Him with a cry of intercession: "LORD, why does Your wrath burn hot against Your people whom You have brought out of the land of Egypt with great power and with a mighty hand?" (verse 11).

"They're *your* people," God essentially said to Moses.

"No, they're *Your* people," Moses basically replied to God.

It was obvious that neither Moses nor God wanted these people in the condition they were in at that particular moment: naked and dancing around a golden calf. When Moses came down to the camp and saw this horrible spectacle, he, in righteous indignation, smashed the tablets God had given him.

The next day, Moses started back up the mountain with great determination in his heart. When he reached the top, he began to speak to God. The statement the burdened prophet made to Him is very significant. It is a sigh, a groan, a cry. It is a sentence that has no ending. Even in the King James Version, the translators left the end of the sentence trailing, using a dash for punctuation. You might say it was a sentence that was broken in the middle by the sobs of a man who was asking to be sent to hell . . . if only the people might be spared the righteous indignation of a holy God: "Then Moses returned to the LORD and said, 'Oh, these people have committed a great sin, and have made for themselves a god of gold! Yet now, if You will forgive their sin —'" (verses 31–32).

At this point, the sentence stops and the translators end it with a dash. It must have been a long pause, as Moses was no doubt considering the full implications of what he was asking. He went on to say, "But if not, I pray, blot me out of Your book which You have written" (verse 32).

As you can see, Moses had a tremendous burden for the people he was praying for, and he was willing to stand in the gap. God, speaking of His desire to find people with such a burden, said, "I sought for a man among them who would make a wall, and stand in the gap before Me on behalf of the land, that I should not destroy it; but I found no one" (Ezekiel 22:30).

The great Christian writer Alexander McClaren penned these words: "Tell me the depth of a Christian's compassion, and I will tell you the measure of his usefulness."

FLEXIBILITY IS KEY

> When I am with those who are weak, I share their weakness, for I want to bring the weak to Christ. Yes, I try to find common ground with everyone, doing everything I can to save some. I do everything to spread the Good News and share in its blessings. (1 Corinthians 9:22–23, NLT)

We could sum up this aspect of evangelism in one word: flexibility. You need to adapt yourself to other people. Jesus is our supreme example in this. Have you ever noticed that He never spoke to any two people in exactly the same way? He saw people as individuals. Some Christians share the great truths of the gospel as if it were coming off a teleprompter. They simply regurgitate all the information they have memorized. Memorizing Scripture, knowing what you believe, and being able to present it effectively is right and good, but we also need to be sensitive to the people we are speaking to.

When Jesus talked to Pontius Pilate, the Roman leader asked him questions. Jesus responded to Pilate's interest. He spoke to Pilate about truth. But when Jesus was brought before Herod, He remained silent. Jesus saw genuine curiosity in Pilate and responded accordingly. In contrast, Jesus knew Herod had no real interest in spiritual things. Herod wanted to be dazzled, not changed. We, too, need to be discerning and refrain from offering the truths of God to someone who is not actually interested.

Jesus made these distinctions when He talked to other people as well. When Nicodemus came to Him and said, "No one can do these signs that You do unless God is with him" (John 3:2), Jesus got straight to the point and in essence said, "Look, Nicodemus, let's get down to brass tacks: You must be born again."

There are times when God will have us do the same. I have walked up to complete strangers and said, "Has anyone ever told you about Jesus Christ? I would like to share Him with you."

There have been other times, however, when I have felt it was best not to take that approach. We see this with Jesus and the Samaritan woman. He sat down at a well in Samaria as she came to draw water at noon. She chose to make her trip to the well at that time of day because she was an outcast of society. She had been divorced a number of times and was presently living with a man she wasn't married to. And not only that, she was a Samaritan.

In those days, many of the Jews looked down on Samaritans because of racial prejudice. Nevertheless, Jesus walked over to the well and sat down. As the woman was drawing water, Jesus asked her for a drink.

She turned and looked at Him in amazement, saying, "How is it that You, being a Jew, ask a drink from me, a Samaritan woman?" (John 4:9).

Then Jesus threw out a little bait by saying, "If you knew the gift of God, and who it is who says to you, 'Give Me a drink,' you would have asked Him, and He would have given you living water" (verse 10).

Having caught her interest, she then responded, "Where then do You get that living water?" (verse 11).

There are times I have found this to work very well. In the course of a conversation with a nonbeliever, I might say, "I'm glad that God is in control of my life." That will usually get a little reaction. One eyebrow goes up, they look at their watch, and perhaps go on their way as quickly as possible. Or, they might say, "What do you mean, 'God is in control of your life'?" These types of statements can act as bait to get someone's attention. If the person is interested, you can then go a little further.

USE TACT

A good example of the right way to witness comes from the story of Philip and the Ethiopian eunuch, which we looked at earlier in this chapter. The Ethiopian had come to Jerusalem searching for God, but sadly he didn't find Him in the empty religion of the day. He did, however, pick up one very valuable item during his visit. He obtained a scroll containing the book of Isaiah. During his ride home, he was reading aloud from Isaiah 53, one of the great messianic chapters that speaks of Jesus.

At this time, God directed Philip to this powerful, wealthy, yet empty and searching man. The way Philip approached him is a good illustration of using tact.

Tact is intuitively knowing how to say the right thing at the right time. Philip simply said to this man, "Do you understand what you are reading?" He could have said, "Did you know that you are going to be judged by God and thrown into hell? What do you think about that?" But because Philip was sensitive to this man's need, he had an open door to share the gospel.

HAVE SOME HEART

Another aspect of effective witnessing involves the heart. When Jesus came into contact with people, He genuinely loved them. He took an interest in them. Heartfelt concern will speak volumes to someone before you even utter a word. There are so few people who really care anymore. Everyone seems to have ulterior motives — they want something from you. As a result, we have a world that is suspicious of anyone who talks with them.

Once I was given two tickets to Disneyland. Because I was meeting some friends inside the park, I didn't need two tickets — I only needed one. As I walked in, I began to feel guilty that I was wasting a free ticket. After all, maybe there was someone who really wanted to go into the park but couldn't afford it. So I left and found some kids in the parking lot and offered the ticket to them. Their response was typical of anyone who has grown cynical about "free" offers: "What do you mean? Why are you giving me that ticket?" They didn't want it. It took nearly thirty minutes before I finally found someone who was willing to take the ticket.

The world today is flooded with religious cults. Satan is no fool. He has put so many imitations out there that non-believers are suspicious of anyone who talks about God.

These counterfeit Christians are out in full force in airports, malls, and on the streets, sharing what they perceive to be the truth. We may not like what they are saying or the way they are misrepresenting God, yet we must ask ourselves, *When was the last time I properly represented God?*

Jesus truly loved people, and we must do the same. That is our edge. The cults don't have Jesus' real love for people. We, however, have His love operating in our lives, because "the love of God has been poured out in our hearts by the Holy Spirit who was given to us" (Romans 5:5).

ONE OF YOUR MOST POWERFUL TOOLS

You already possess one of the most effective tools for communicating your faith: your testimony (how you came to know Christ personally). If you go through the book of Acts and read some of the great evangelistic messages of the apostle Paul, you will find that he often used his personal testimony. Certainly his was a dramatic one, but God can also use your personal testimony because it is unique.

Through your personal testimony, you can relay thoughts and feelings that others can easily relate to. Having established that common ground, you can then share how God has worked in your life. In this way, you come back to the central message: Jesus Christ and His cross.

Once you have the opportunity to share the gospel, it's important to point people to Scripture. But which verses should you share? At the back of this book (starting on page 113), I have included "The Plan of Salvation," which includes key verses you might want to memorize.

TRUE DISCIPLESHIP

The full concept of discipleship is to share our faith, lead people to Christ, and then help them mature. But somewhere along the line, we have separated evangelism from discipleship. There is no such distinction in Scripture, however. The idea is not just to pray with someone and send them on their way. It is to help that new believer grow spiritually and become a dedicated, committed, fruitful, and mature disciple of Jesus Christ. And then we encourage that new believer to repeat the process with someone else. And so the cycle continues.

After Saul's conversion, there was great doubt among the believers as to whether he had really come to genuine faith in Christ. After all, Saul was one of the prime persecutors of the early church. He presided over the first execution of a Christian in the New Testament, a young man named Stephen. Upon hearing that the notorious Saul had become a believer, the disciples were afraid it was just a ploy—a ruse to find out where they met so he could turn them over to the authorities. But God spoke to a man named Ananias and told him to go and visit Saul. Ananias obeyed, found Saul (who later changed his name to Paul), and took the time to pray for him and encourage him (see Acts 9:10–19).

Then God brought a man named Barnabas into Paul's life. Barnabas introduced Paul to the apostles and personally reassured them that Paul's conversion was sincere.

This is a good illustration of true discipleship. Discipling someone isn't just downloading a bunch of information; it is also being a friend. Sadly, I find that many people who accept Christ often fall through the cracks because no one helps them become established in the faith. It can be difficult for these people to get acclimated to church.

New believers may come to church for the first time and be encouraged by the warmth and friendliness, but when the Bible study starts and they hear something like, "Turn to Matthew 5," they immediately feel lost because they don't have the faintest idea where to look.

That's exactly how I felt when I began attending church. I remember how I didn't understand the language of Christians. They had their own unique vocabulary—you might call it *Christianese*. I thank God that a believer saw me and took me under his wing. He invited me to church and introduced me to his Christian friends. After the services, he explained what different things meant and answered my questions.

When we lead someone to Christ or meet a new Christian, we must take the initiative to see that they are stabilized in their newfound faith. Take them to church, introduce them to friends, and, most importantly, be a friend.

New believers not only need to hear the truth; they need to see it lived. They can't necessarily get that from a pulpit. They need to see it in the lifestyle of a person in day-to-day living. Obviously, they will have many questions: How does a Christian act at work? How does a Christian behave behind the wheel? How does a Christian treat his or her spouse and family? How does a Christian spend free time? What movies does a Christian see? These are all a part of the discipleship process.

One thing that keeps Christians from being active disciples is the fear of not knowing enough about the Bible. It isn't necessary that you be a Bible scholar to lead others to Christ and disciple them. Remember, you probably know a lot more than a brand-new believer does. You can begin by sharing the building blocks of the Christian life that this book talks about: how to study the Bible, how to pray, the importance of involvement in the church, and how to live a godly life. Your life can impact a new believer's life in a powerful, transformational way.

BENEFITS OF DISCIPLEMAKING

The discipling of others is extremely important in the life of a disciple, because the failure to do so will have damaging results on your own walk with Christ. Attending more Bible studies, more prayer meetings, reading more Christian books, and listening to more teaching without an outlet for the truth will cause us to spiritually decay. We need to take what God has given us and use it constructively in the lives of others.

When you take a new believer under your wing, you are not only encouraging a new child of God, but you are saving *yourself* from spiritual stagnation. New believers need our wisdom, knowledge, and experience, and we need the zeal, spark, and childlike simplicity of faith that a young Christian possesses.

Have you ever led anyone to Jesus Christ? Have you discipled anyone? Have you taken any new believer under your wing and helped him or her along? If you do, it will reignite your spiritual life as that person discovers the truths of God for the first time (and as you rediscover them too).

When a new believer discovers things from God's Word and we see the excitement it brings, it reignites us. Often they will ask difficult questions that will make us search the Scriptures for answers. And there are always things we have learned but forgotten. A new believer's questions can help us to rediscover (or discover for the first time) many important spiritual truths.

The fact is, many mature Christians come to a point where they simply dry up. When this happens, many begin wondering what is wrong with them. Some seek a solution in finding a new church or some new teaching that supposedly will revolutionize their lives. In most cases, the real problem is simply spiritual sluggishness. The person in this position should be passing along what he or she has learned to a younger believer. We have a choice: either evangelize or fossilize.

Jesus said that "whoever has [or is passing it on] will be given more, and they will have an abundance. Whoever does not have [or is not passing it on], even what they have will be taken from them" (Matthew 13:12, NIV). I have found that the more I give, the more God seems to give back to me.

Just as Jesus said, "The harvest truly is plentiful, but the laborers are few" (Matthew 9:37). We need more laborers, more disciples. May God help you and me to be just that.

DISCIPLESHIP: IT'S YOUR CHOICE

You were placed on earth to know God.

Everything else is secondary.

Your career, your possessions, your friends and family, even your ministries are all a distant second to knowing God. Jesus prayed for His disciples, "This is eternal life, that they may know You, the only true God, and Jesus Christ whom You have sent" (John 17:3).

God said to Jeremiah: "Let not the wise man glory in his wisdom, let not the mighty man glory in his might, nor let the rich man glory in his riches; but let him who glories glory in this, that he understands and knows Me" (Jeremiah 9:23–24).

This was the objective of the apostle Paul, who said, "I want to know Christ—yes, to know the power of his resurrection and participation in his sufferings, becoming like him in his death" (Philippians 3:10, NIV). Another translation states, "That I may progressively become more deeply and intimately acquainted with Him" (AMP).

TOTAL COMMITMENT

A person's last words can sometimes be his or her most significant words. Here is what King David said to his son Solomon from his deathbed:

> "Solomon, my son, learn to know the God of your ancestors intimately. Worship and serve him with your whole heart and a willing mind. For the Lord sees every heart and knows every plan and thought. If you seek him, you will find him. But if you forsake him, he will reject you forever."
> (1 Chronicles 28:9, NLT)

David knew what he was talking about.

When he was just a boy, he had been plucked from obscurity to become the king of Israel. One has only to read the book of Psalms, most of which David penned, to discover that he loved God deeply. He was a young man who enjoyed an extraordinary intimacy with God. That is why the Bible describes him as "a man after [God's] own heart" (1 Samuel 13:14). We read of him tending his sheep out in the fields and singing beautiful songs of praise to God as he played his stringed instrument.

David enjoyed closeness with God and had no idea as he tended his sheep that God would one day call him to become the next king of Israel.

Of course, he had many challenges to face before he ascended the throne. But when his day finally came, he ruled well and with wisdom. He was a courageous warrior and was well-loved by the people. God had blessed him.

But then . . . David started to slip.

The intimacy and closeness we read about in the early phases of his life became less and less evident. He seemed bored and distracted. In fact, on the fateful night when he fell into sin with Bathsheba, we read, "At the time when kings go out to battle . . . David remained at Jerusalem" (2 Samuel 11:1).

Terrible decision!

Instead of being out in the fields leading his troops into battle, he was kicking back and taking a little R & R. Restless and at loose ends, he went up on his rooftop . . . and fell into the worst trouble of his life.

Beautiful Bathsheba was bathing in the cool twilight across the way, and David took advantage of his palace's commanding position in that neighborhood to spy on her. The Bible doesn't fault Bathsheba; it clearly places the blame at the feet of this young king. He was responsible for his actions. When he could have and should have turned away, he didn't.

David brought Bathsheba into his chambers, had sexual relations with her, and she became pregnant. But instead of acknowledging his sin, he had her husband, Uriah, brought back from the battle line to make it appear as though the child were his. But Uriah didn't sleep with his wife, so David basically had Uriah put to death, covered it up (or so he thought), and then married Bathsheba.

David actually thought he had pulled it off. A year passed in which he was out of fellowship with God. Then one day the prophet Nathan confronted David, and he came clean, admitting that he had sinned.

In spite of this tragic fall into sin, the Bible tells us that David was a man after God's own heart. Why is that? Didn't he commit some serious sins? Absolutely. But when he was confronted with his sin, he admitted it. He didn't minimize his sin, blame it on others, or label it as something else. He didn't tell Nathan, "I've made some personal mistakes." He owned up to the horror of what he had done, saying to the prophet, "I have sinned against the LORD" (2 Samuel 12:13).

If you want to be a man or woman after God's own heart, know this: You will sin. You will fall short. But when you realize you have sinned, don't blame others, don't minimize or gloss over what you've done, and don't make excuses for yourself. Say, like David, "Against You, You only, have I sinned, and done this evil in Your sight" (Psalm 51:4). God will forgive you if you will confess your sin to Him (see 1 John 1:9).

Of course, that doesn't mean you won't reap the consequences of that sin in the years to come. David certainly did. Although God forgave him, David saw, to his great sorrow, his own behavior repeated in the lives of his children. He was a man who had learned his lessons in the school of hard knocks.

So when he realized his life was drawing to a close, he essentially told Solomon, "Son, I'm on my way out of here. You will be taking over. Here is what I have learned: *You need to know God.* If you understand this, everything else will fall into place. Solomon, you can't live off my relationship with God. You must develop your own."

Note that David told Solomon to "worship and serve [God] with your whole heart and a willing mind" (1 Chronicles 28:9, NLT). Or as another translation puts it, "Serve [God] with wholehearted devotion and with a willing mind" (NIV). In other words, we need a total commitment to God.

God doesn't want us to follow Him with a divided heart. He wants our complete commitment. It would be like saying to your spouse, "Honey, I love you, but I'm thinking of dating other people. Are you good with that?" Of course not. No one in their right mind would accept such an arrangement.

As for Solomon, he followed his father's advice . . . in the beginning.

The Lord blessed him with great wealth, wisdom, and honor. He was even able to build a temple for the Lord that his father had wanted to build.

As time passed, however, Solomon got away from knowing God. He followed in the *wrong* footsteps of David (rather than the right ones) and, in some ways, made even more tragic mistakes. At the end of it all, after he had compromised his commitment to God and wasted so many great opportunities to lead His people in the fear of the Lord, he finally came back around to bottom-line reality. He wrote these words: "Here now is my final conclusion: Fear God and obey his commands, for this is everyone's duty" (Ecclesiastes 12:13, NLT).

It was too late to undo so much of the damage he had done, but I believe Solomon came to recognize the wisdom of his father's strong counsel to know and follow God.

HOW TO KNOW GOD

So how do you do that? How do you come to know God?

Actually, we've been learning the essentials of knowing God—the essentials of discipleship—throughout this book.

1. We know God through the careful study of His Word. It is in the Bible that we discover the character and nature of God. It is in the Bible that we learn about what is right and wrong, about what is good and evil.

We don't discover these things by voting on them or by what is currently acceptable in our culture. It would do no good at all to take a national poll and capture the majority opinion. We discover truths about God by studying His Word. And if you begin to neglect this, your spiritual life ultimately will start unraveling. Everything you need to know about God is found in the Bible.

2. We know God through prayer. We need to get past the formalities and gain a true understanding of what prayer is about. The objective of prayer isn't to get God to do what we want Him to do; it is to get us to do what God wants us to do. It is to align our will with His. If you can discover that, then your prayers will start being answered more often in the affirmative. Seek to spend time in prayer, because that is how you are going to know God.

3. We know God through worship. Worship is far more than something we do when we gather with other believers and sing songs of praise.

The word *worship* has its origins in the old English word *worthship*. It means to ascribe value or worth to someone or something. In describing heaven, the apostle John wrote,

> Then I looked, and I heard the voice of many angels around the throne, the living creatures, and the elders; and the number of them was ten thousand times ten thousand, and thousands of thousands, saying with a loud voice:
>
> "Worthy is the Lamb who was slain
> To receive power and riches and wisdom,
> And strength and honor and glory and
> blessing!" (Revelation 5:11-12)

We worship God because He is worthy — not because we are in the mood to worship.

4. We know God through fellowship with other believers. The first-century believers met on a regular basis, not just once a week. I have never understood Christians who think, *I'm going to make my appearance once a week, and that will be the extent of it.* If that is your focus, then you are missing out on something. There is so much more.

When we read about the church in the New Testament, we see that they met regularly — and with passion. They "continued steadfastly" (Acts 2:42). They were there, helping out and loving and knowing God.

IT STARTS WITH US

As we approach the end of this book, I want to underscore something one more time: *The more we know God, the more we should want to make Him known to a lost world.* As we look at our world today, as we look at our nation, it's easy for us to say, "America needs revival."

But let's narrow it down.

Revival starts with you and me.

We need to revisit 2 Chronicles 7:14, where God says,

> "If My people who are called by My name will humble themselves, and pray and seek My face, and turn from their wicked ways, then I will hear from heaven, and will forgive their sin and heal their land."

Linger over the words of this verse. Commit it to memory. We all want to see our land healed. But notice that God directs His words to *His* people. God doesn't point His finger at Congress or the State House or the White House. He doesn't point His finger at Hollywood. He says, "If *My* people . . ." We need to ask God if there is anything in our lives that isn't right with Him. That is where we need to be looking right now.

God says, "For I know the thoughts that I think toward you . . . thoughts of peace and not of evil, to give you a future and a hope" (Jeremiah 29:11). The word *future* also could be translated "an expected end" or "hope in your final outcome" (AMP).

In other words, there will be an outcome, a completion in your life. God will tie up the loose ends. As a Christian, you're still a work in progress. But the Bible assures us that "He who has begun a good work in you will complete it until the day of Jesus Christ" (Philippians 1:6).

I'm an artist. I like to draw and design and have always been interested in graphics. There have been times when I'm drawing something, and someone will look over my shoulder and ask, "What's it going to be?"

"Just wait," I say.

"I think you should do this. . . ."

"No," I tell them, "just let me do it. When I'm finished, I'd be happy to show it to you. *But not yet.*"

In the same way, each of us is a work in progress. God is doing a work in your life, and when it's done, He'll show you. But it is not done yet, so be patient. God sees the end from the beginning. Ecclesiastes 3:11 says, "He has made everything beautiful in its time. Also He has put eternity in their hearts, except that no one can find out the work that God does from beginning to end."

We can't see the work God is doing, but that doesn't mean He isn't working! One wonderful day in the future, we will be free from the effects of sin, and we no longer will experience the limitations of the human body. We won't have any more unanswered questions, and we will live forever in the presence of God Almighty.

In the meantime, we should make it our aim to live godly lives, which means doing what God tells us to do. The simple fact is that we have no right to say we know God if we don't seek to live the way He has called us to live.

Talk is cheap. I believe in verbally proclaiming the gospel, but our lifestyle is vitally important. Many times our words carry no weight because we contradict them by the way we live. As 1 John 2:3–4 reminds us, "We can be sure that we know him if we obey his commandments. If someone claims, 'I know God,' but doesn't obey God's commandments, that person is a liar and is not living in the truth" (NLT).

This means that as Christians, we ought to tell the truth.

It means we shouldn't steal anything—not even our employer's time.

It means we should keep our marriage vows.

It means we will strive to be men and women of integrity, because we know that people are watching us.

It's amazing how many people will say they know God, but refuse to do what He says. As I pointed out earlier, you are the only Bible some people will ever read. When we are living godly lives, it earns us the right to proclaim the gospel boldly. People can see we are changed, and for that reason, they will be far more open to hearing our message.

SAVED SOUL, WASTED LIFE

As a young man, Alan Redpath was a successful CPA. He had made a commitment to Christ, but he wasn't really living for the Lord as he should have been. One day, he was talking with a Christian friend who made a statement that would alter the course of his life.

His friend said, "It is possible to have a saved soul and a wasted life."

Redpath couldn't forget those words. They haunted him all that day, into the night, and throughout the next day. He couldn't let them go. He realized that God was showing him that he had a saved soul but a *wasted life*. So Redpath dropped to his knees and prayed, "Lord, I want Your will for me. I don't want to waste my life. I dedicate it to You." God redirected his course, and instead of being a CPA, Redpath became a minister and served God for many years—which included writing a number of wonderful Christian books.

I'm not suggesting that if you dedicate your life to God, He will redirect you to become a minister or a missionary, although He could. He might leave you right where you are, but show you a new way to use your gifts for His glory. Then again, He might direct you to take another path you have never even considered.

But here is what it comes down to: Your life belongs to God. You don't share your time and talents with Him; He shares them with you! He owns you and everything about you. You need to recognize and acknowledge that fact.

The attitude of a true disciple should be, "Lord, I don't know how much time I have left. I may have many years. Or, I may not have as many as I hope to have. Either way, my time is in Your hands. I dedicate myself to You. You have given me the sacred trust of getting the gospel message out. I'm ready to do my part."

Are you willing to make this commitment today?

A VERY IMPORTANT FINAL WORD

Have you ever wondered why God put you on this earth in the first place? Have you ever thought about the reasons God created you or what your purpose in life might be?

Our primary purpose in life is to know and love God.

The book of Revelation tells us that God "created all things, and by [His] will they were created and have their being" (Revelation 4:11, NIV). What a thought! God has called us, before everything else, to know Him personally and to walk with Him, with the amazing by-product of actually bringing Him pleasure. (I'll let you in on a little secret: It will bring you pleasure as well.)

Do you know God today?

Maybe you can't say with absolute assurance that you do. That is a terribly important realization to make, because if you don't know God today, He won't know you in that final day when you stand before Him. If you want to be sure you

111

will go to heaven, you must have this relationship with God. There has to be a moment in your life when you say, "I am a sinner. I am sorry for that sin." There has to be a moment in your life when you turn from that sin and put your faith in Jesus Christ as your Savior and Lord.

If you haven't done that, will you do it today? Simply say a prayer like this one, and mean it in your heart: "Dear Lord Jesus, I know I am a sinner. I believe You died for my sins. Right now, I turn from my sins and open the door of my heart and life. I confess You as my personal Lord and Savior. Thank You for saving me. Amen."

The Bible tells us, "If we confess our sins, He is faithful and just to forgive us our sins and to cleanse us from all unrighteousness" (1 John 1:9). If you just prayed that prayer and meant it, Jesus Christ has now taken residence in your heart. Your decision to follow Christ means God has forgiven you and you will spend eternity in heaven.

To help you grow in your newfound faith, be sure to make the following a part of your life each day: reading the Bible, praying, spending time with other Christians by going to church, and telling others about your faith in Christ.

For additional resources to help you learn more about what it means to be a follower of Jesus Christ, please visit www.harvest.org/knowgod/.

THE PLAN OF SALVATION

1. The Condition: We Are All Sinners

The first thing we need to establish with those whom we share the gospel is the fact that we are all sinners. One word that defines sin is the Greek word *harmatia*, which means "to miss the mark." What is God's mark? Perfection. Jesus said, "Be perfect, therefore, as your heavenly Father is perfect" (Matthew 5:48, NIV). Apart from God, no one is perfect; everyone has missed the mark. Therefore, everyone is a sinner.

- **1 John 1:8–9:** "If we say that we have no sin, we deceive ourselves, and the truth is not in us. If we confess our sins, He is faithful and just to forgive us our sins and to cleanse us from all unrighteousness."
- **Romans 3:23:** "For all have sinned and fall short of the glory of God."

- **Isaiah 53:6:** "All we like sheep have gone astray; we have turned, every one, to his own way; and the LORD has laid on Him the iniquity of us all."

2. The Result: Death

Next, we need to establish the result of sin. Every one of us has missed God's mark. Every one of us has fallen short of being perfect. The result of that is death. We are getting only what we deserve, and we are bringing that judgment upon ourselves. One thing we need to remember is that God does not send anyone to hell. We send ourselves there by rejecting His truth.

- **Romans 6:23:** "For the wages of sin is death, but the gift of God is eternal life in Christ Jesus our Lord."

3. The Solution: Christ's Death on the Cross

At this point, let people know the solution: Christ died for our sins.

- **John 3:16–17:** "For God so loved the world that He gave His only begotten Son, that whoever believes in Him should not perish but have everlasting life. For God did not send His Son into the world to condemn the world, but that the world through Him might be saved."
- **Isaiah 53:5:** "But He was wounded for our transgressions, He was bruised for our iniquities; the chastisement for our peace was upon Him, and by His stripes we are healed."
- **Romans 5:8:** "But God demonstrates His own love toward us, in that while we were still sinners, Christ died for us."

Since we can never measure up to God's standards on our own, God has reached out to us. We cannot solve the problem of sin, but God, who is perfect, can and has. He has become a bridge for us through Jesus Christ.

4. The Choice: To Accept or Reject Jesus Christ as Savior

If someone will acknowledge they are sinners and accept the premise that Christ is the solution, they are at a crossroads. Either they can reject God's solution and accept the consequences, or they can accept Jesus Christ as Savior. What must they do to be forgiven of their sins and come into a relationship with God? First, they must repent.

- **Luke 13:3:** " 'I tell you, no; but unless you repent you will all likewise perish.' "
- **Acts 3:19:** "Repent therefore and be converted, that your sins may be blotted out, so that times of refreshing may come from the presence of the Lord."
- **Acts 17:30:** "Truly, these times of ignorance God overlooked, but now commands all men everywhere to repent."

Upon the realization that they are sinners and having repented of that sin, they must then come to Jesus Christ.

- **Matthew 11:28–30:** " 'Come to Me, all you who labor and are heavy laden, and I will give you rest. Take My yoke upon you and learn from Me, for I am gentle and lowly in heart, and you will find rest for your souls. For My yoke is easy and My burden is light.' "

5. The Response: To Receive the Gift of Eternal Life

Christ's invitation is clear. We must come to Him. All that remains is a response.

- **Romans 6:23:** "For the wages of sin is death, but the gift of God is eternal life in Christ Jesus our Lord."

What must we do to receive God's gift of salvation? Take it!

- **Revelation 3:20:** "Behold, I stand at the door and knock. If anyone hears My voice and opens the door, I will come in to him and dine with him, and he with Me."

Jesus stands at the door of your heart and mine and knocks, seeking entrance into our lives. What do we have to do to let Him in? Open the door!

- **John 1:12:** "But as many as received Him, to them He gave the right to become children of God, to those who believe in His name."

We must receive Him. How? By asking Him into our lives. If we have shared these truths with someone who then wants to receive Christ, we need only to extend the invitation. In fact, we should pray with them at that very moment if they would like to make this life-changing decision to receive and follow Jesus Christ. I know of no greater joy than leading someone in a prayer to receive Christ.

6. The Assurance of Salvation

Following this, it is important that a new believer has the assurance that Christ has come into his or her life.

- **1 John 5:11–13:** "And this is the testimony: that God has given us eternal life, and this life is in His Son. He who has the Son has life; he who does not have the Son of God does not have life. These things I have written to you who believe in the name of the Son of God, that you may know that you have eternal life, and that you may continue to believe in the name of the Son of God."
- **2 Corinthians 5:17:** "Therefore, if anyone is in Christ, he is a new creation; old things have passed away; behold, all things have become new."
- **Psalm 103:12:** "As far as the east is from the west, so far has He removed our transgressions from us."

7. The Profession of Faith

At this time, you may encourage a new believer to make a public confession of his or her newfound faith in Christ.

- **Matthew 10:32–33:** " 'Therefore whoever confesses Me before men, him I will also confess before My Father who is in heaven. But whoever denies Me before men, him I will also deny before My Father who is in heaven.' "

After you have led someone to Christ, it is important to take them under your wing and help them get established in their relationship with Christ.

QUESTIONS FOR DISCUSSION

Chapter 1: Are You His Disciple?

1. Read again Hebrews 6:1 and 1 Peter 2:1–3. What does the Bible say about "growing up" in our salvation and not remaining spiritual babies?

2. When Jesus said, "Follow Me," in Mark 2:14, He literally meant "Follow *with* Me." What's the difference between those two commands? How could "Follow with Me" be both a command and an encouraging promise?

3. Look again at Luke 14:26–28, 33. Is Jesus really asking us to *hate* our family and friends? What is His real message to us here?

4. In your own words, explain this statement: "Either you will have harmony with God and friction with people, or you will have harmony with people and friction with God."

5. Jesus said, "If anyone desires to come after Me, let him deny himself, and take up his cross daily, and follow Me"

(Luke 9:23). What does it mean for you and me to "take up [our] cross daily"?

Chapter 2: Traits of a Disciple

1. What does it mean in John 15:4 when Jesus says, "Abide in Me, and I in you"? How does abiding in Christ day by day, hour by hour, affect our response to the situations and circumstances of our lives?

2. Why should it be our goal to have a "steadfast spirit," as David prayed for in Psalm 51:10?

3. What is the danger of substituting activity *for* God for time *with* God? How do we fall into this trap? How can we avoid it?

4. In Acts 4:13, we read that when Peter and John stood before the Sanhedrin, the Jewish leaders "realized that they had been with Jesus." What do you think tipped them off? How can people in your life tell that you have "been with Jesus"?

5. What did Jesus mean when He said, "Woe to you when everyone speaks well of you" (Luke 6:26, NIV). Why should being liked by everyone and well thought of by everyone tip us off that something might be wrong in our Christian life?

Chapter 3: The Costs of Discipleship

1. What does the author mean when he says there is a price tag associated with following Jesus? What are some of the specific costs we must face if we want to be His disciple?

2. In Mark 14:3–9, Mary of Bethany was showing extravagant love when she poured out a whole bottle of highly expensive perfume on Jesus. What motivated her to do that? How did Jesus defend her when she was criticized?

What are some ways we can show extravagant love for our Lord and Savior?

3. The author writes, "No, you can't do everything, but you can do something. . . . *So do what you can.* We all have something that we can do. And we must all do what we can while we can." In view of all Jesus has done for us, what are some of the things we can do for Him right here, right now?

4. Read 1 Corinthians 6:19–20. Thinking of your own life, what are some of the biggest implications of these verses? How would your life change if you allowed your life to be guided by these truths every day?

5. In Hebrews 12:1 we read, "Let us strip off every weight that slows us down, especially the sin that so easily trips us up" (NLT). What are some of the weights that slow us down in our desire to be disciples of Jesus? What are some of the sins that so easily trip us up?

Chapter 4: Discipleship and the Bible

1. To get the most out of Scripture, we must receive and treasure it. In a practical sense, how can you and I treasure the words of the Bible in our lives?

2. The author writes, "We are better off reading five verses slowly and understanding what they mean than reading five chapters quickly and not getting anything out of them." What are some of the ways we can slow down and get more out of what we are reading in Scripture?

3. Colossians 3:16 says, "Let the word of Christ dwell in you richly." The author notes that the passage could be translated, "Let the word of Christ *permeate* your life" or "Let the word of Christ be at home inside of you." What

are some practical ways we can do that?

4. What is the value of actually disciplining ourselves to learn verses from the Bible by heart?

5. The author writes, "It is not enough to go through the Word of God; the Word of God must go through us. It is not how we mark our Bible; it is how our Bible marks us." What are some ways we can apply God's Word to our own lives and situations? How can we make sure Scripture will really impact what we do, say, and think?

Chapter 5: Discipleship and Prayer

1. If God knows what we need, why doesn't He give us everything in one big weekly (or monthly) bundle? Why does He want us to come to Him day by day with our needs and requests?

2. The author writes that the Lord's Prayer (Matthew 6:9-13) should really be called the Disciples' Prayer. Why is that? How is this prayer a *guide* for us, rather than something we should always repeat word for word?

3. *"Our Father in heaven, hallowed be Your name."* Why is it important for us to think about who we are praying to before we turn to Him with our requests?

4. The author writes, "A person can't really pray, 'Your kingdom come,' until he or she can first pray, 'My kingdom go.'" What do you think he means by this? As you consider this, what are the implications for your own life?

5. We read in this chapter that most unanswered prayers are outside the will of God. How can we begin to align our prayers more closely to God's will for our lives?

Chapter 6: Discipleship and the Church

1. The Bible tells us to "think of ways to motivate one another to acts of love and good works. And let us not neglect our meeting together, as some people do, but encourage one another" (Hebrews 10:24–25, NLT). What does this passage say happens when Christians gather regularly in church? What, then, would be the result if we neglected to do this?

2. The chapter says, "The number-one priority in selecting a church should not be how close it is to your home or how nice its facilities are." What, then, *is* the number-one priority?

3. The chapter tells us that the more we *give* to others in the context of our participation in a healthy church, the more capacity we will find in ourselves to *receive* what God has for us. Describe how this might work in your life. How do you receive by giving yourself away in Christ?

4. Normal Christian living as presented in the New Testament was a passionate, Spirit-empowered, all-consuming devotion to God and to His Word. If that was first-century normal, what is today's normal? How can we as believers return to New Testament normal?

5. According to this chapter, authentic fellowship isn't just Christian social activity — gab sessions with cookies and coffee. What are some aspects of the true and deeper meaning of fellowship, or *koinonia*, between believers?

Chapter 7: Discipling Others

1. Read again Matthew 28:18–20. Why is this the Great Commission rather than a great suggestion? Do most

believers take these words of Jesus as more of an optional activity or good idea, or do they receive them as a command?

2. In Acts 4:29, how did the disciples respond to the threats and intimidation of the authorities to keep quiet about Jesus? What did they specifically pray for? Are you willing to pray as they prayed, in the face of indifference or opposition to your witness? What might happen in your day if you prayed this each morning?

3. The author writes, "The hardest thing about sharing your faith with unbelievers is getting started, forcing those first words out of your mouth." Why do you think that might be? Why might that conversation get easier once you get the ball rolling?

4. Jesus says to His disciples, "You are the salt of the earth." A distinct quality of salt is that it affects everything it comes into contact with. In what ways can we be "salt" in our job . . . in our neighborhood . . . in our school . . . in our family?

5. Another quality of salt is that it makes people thirsty. Read Colossians 4:5–6. How can we use even casual conversation with people to make them thirsty to know more about God, who loves them?

Chapter 8: Discipleship: It's Your Choice

1. "You were placed on earth to know God. Everything else is secondary . . . a distant second to knowing God." Looking back on your life over the last weeks, could you honestly say that about yourself? What steps could you take to adjust your priorities?

2. Both David and Solomon started out in life loving the

Lord passionately and making right decisions. Yet both of them drifted from God later, disappointing many and bringing trouble on themselves and their families. What causes Christians to drift away from the truth and their love for the Lord? How can we prevent that drift in our own lives?

3. The author writes, "We discover truths about God by studying His Word. And if you begin to neglect this, your spiritual life ultimately will start unraveling." What are some practical ways you can discipline yourself to read, study, and meditate on the Bible every day?

4. "The objective of prayer isn't to get God to do what we want Him to do." What, then, *is* the objective of prayer? How does prayer change both our circumstances and *ourselves* as we give it priority in our day?

5. We can't always see the work God is doing in our lives, but that doesn't mean He isn't working! Read Philippians 1:6; 2:12–13; Romans 8:28–29; and Hebrews 13:20–21. What do you see in these verses that encourages you about God and His being active and at work in your life?

NOTES

1. Martin E. Marty, ed., *The Place of Trust: Martin Luther on the Sermon on the Mount* (New York: Harper & Row, 1983), 34.

Other Books by Greg Laurie

Are We Living in the Last Days?
As I See It
Better Than Happiness
Daily Hope for Hurting Hearts
Dealing with Giants
Deepening Your Faith
Discipleship
Essentials
For Every Season, volumes 1, 2, and 3
God's Design for Christian Dating
A Handbook on Christian Dating
His Christmas Presence
Hope for Hurting Hearts
How to Know God
"I'm Going on a Diet Tomorrow"
Living Out Your Faith
Making God Known
Marriage Connections
Married. Happily.
Run to Win
Secrets to Spiritual Success
Signs of the Times
Strengthening Your Faith
Strengthening Your Marriage
Ten Things You Should Know About God and Life
The Great Compromise
The Greatest Stories Ever Told, volumes 1, 2, and 3
Upside Down Living
What Every Christian Needs to Know
Why, God?
Worldview

Visit: www.kerygmapublishing.com